COLLINS

YOUNG READERS' DICTIONARY

David Smith and Susan Cassin

HarperCollins
London · New York · Glasgow · Sydney
Auckland · Toronto · Johannesburg

First published as Collins Early Dictionary 1984
© text 1984, 1985 David Smith and Sue Cassin
© illustrations 1984, 1985, William Collins Sons and Co Ltd

This edition published 1991 by HarperCollins

A CIP catalogue for this book is available from the British Library

ISBN 0 00 196398 8 (HB)
ISBN 0 00 196397 X (PB)

All rights reserved. No part of this publication may be reproduced, stored in a retrieval system, or transmitted, in any form or by any means, electronic, mechanical, photocopying, recording or otherwise, without the prior permission of the publishers.

Printed and bound in Great Britain by HarperCollins Manufacturing Division, Glasgow.

Contents

how to use this book	4
weather and sky	5
growing things	9
animals and other living creatures	13
my body	43
people	51
food and drink	67
fruit	75
vegetables	78
things we wear	81
at home	91
outside	92
garage	94
garden	96
kitchen	98
living room	104
bathroom	106
bedroom	108
toys	109
we use	115
places and buildings	123
transport	137
action words	143
helpful words	169
where	172
what kind	173
storybook people	177
days	184
months	185
numbers	186
time	187
colours	188
index	192

How to use this dictionary

Dictionaries tell you the meaning of a word. In this dictionary each word is illustrated to help you understand the meaning.

All the words are listed under various topics. If you want to look up **kitten,** and you know that a kitten is an animal, you would look for **animals** in the contents list on the opposite page, turn to where that section starts and look under **k** until you find the word you want.

The words in each topic are listed in alphabetical order. So, in the **animals** topic **a**pe comes before **b**adger, **b**adger comes before **c**ow, **c**ow comes before **d**eer and so on.

Here is the alphabet to help you:

a b c d e f g h i j k l m n o p q r s t u v w x y z

These are the small letters. You will see as you use the dictionary that the first letter of each sentence begins with a differently shaped letter. These are called capital letters.
The capital letters are:

**A B C D E F G H I J K L M N
O P Q R S T U V W X Y Z**

If you are not sure under which topic a word would be listed, go to the index at the back of the book where all the words defined in the book are listed in alphabetical order with a page number alongside. You will find the word you want on that page.

Once you get used to using a dictionary, you will find that you want to use it more and more and that a good dictionary is one of the most important books in your schoolbag or desk.

weather and sky

weather and sky

autumn
Autumn comes after summer.
Many trees lose their leaves in autumn.

cloud
A **cloud** is made of many tiny drops of water.
Clouds float in the sky.

fog
Fog is a thick cloud on the ground. It is difficult to see through **fog**.

frost
Frost is very small drops of frozen water. It makes the ground white.

ice
Ice is frozen water.

lightning
Lightning is a flash of light in the sky when there is a storm.

moon
The **moon** shines in the sky at night.

rain
Rain is drops of water falling from clouds.

rainbow
A **rainbow** has seven colours. We may see a **rainbow** when the sun shines through rain.

sky
The **sky** is the space above the earth. Birds fly in the **sky**.

snow
Snow is frozen water in the air. **Snow** falls in tiny white flakes.

space
The sun, moon and stars are in **space**. Astronauts travel in **space**.

weather and sky

weather and sky

spring
Spring comes after winter. Lambs are born in **spring**.

stars
Stars are the small, bright lights we see in the sky at night. They are very far away.

summer
Summer is the warmest time of the year. It comes after spring.

sun
The **sun** makes the earth warm. It gives us light by day.

thunder
When there is a storm you may hear a loud rumbling noise. This is **thunder**.

winter
Winter is the coldest time of the year. It comes after autumn.

growing things

acorn
An **acorn** is the nut of an oak tree.

bulb
Some flowers grow from a **bulb**. A daffodil grows from a **bulb**.

bush
A **bush** is like a small tree. We can plant **bushes** to make a hedge.

conker
A **conker** is the nut of a horse-chestnut tree.

flower
The bright, coloured petals of a plant make a **flower**.

grass
Grass is a green plant that covers fields and lawns.

leaf
A **leaf** is part of a tree or a plant. Some **leaves** fall in the autumn.

plant
A **plant** grows in the ground or in water.

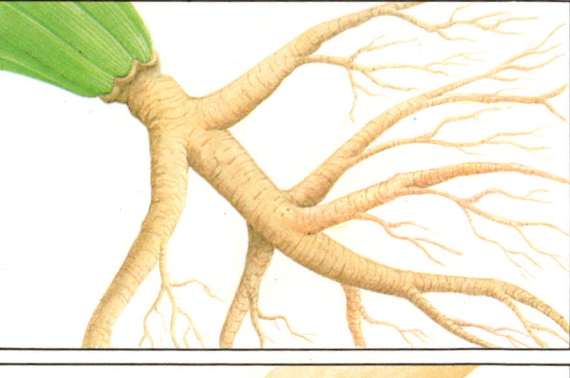

roots
Roots are the parts of a plant that grow under the ground.

seeds
Many plants grow from **seeds**.

growing things

toadstool
A **toadstool** looks like a mushroom. It must not be eaten.

trees
Trees are large plants. They have roots, a trunk, branches and leaves.

animals and other living creatures

animals, living creatures

alligator
An **alligator** is a large reptile that lives near water. It has thick skin and strong jaws.

ant
An **ant** is a small insect that lives in the ground. **Ants** work very hard.

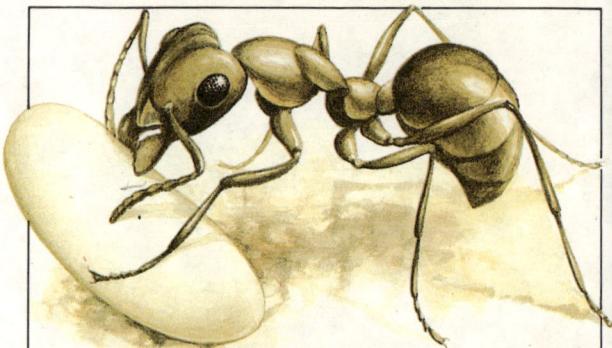

ape
An **ape** is a large animal. **Apes** do not have tails.

badger
A **badger** is a furry animal with short legs and long claws, **Badgers** come out at night.

bat
A **bat** is like a mouse with wings. **Bats** fly when it is getting dark.

bear
A **bear** is a big, heavy animal. It has thick fur.

beaver
A **beaver** lives near water. It has sharp teeth, a flat tail and webbed back feet.

bee
A **bee** is a flying insect. It makes honey.

beetle
A **beetle** is an insect. It has hard skin.

bird
A **bird** has wings and feathers. Most **birds** can fly. They all lay eggs.

bison
A **bison** is a wild ox. It is very strong and heavy.

blackbird
A **blackbird** has a yellow beak.

blue-tit
A **blue-tit** has blue and yellow feathers. **Blue-tits** are garden birds.

brontosaurus
A **brontosaurus** was a dinosaur. It was very big.

budgerigar
A **budgerigar** is often kept as a pet bird. It has brightly coloured feathers.

butterfly
A **butterfly** is an insect which develops from a caterpillar. It has bright, coloured wings.

calf
A **calf** is a baby cow.

camel
A **camel** can carry a heavy load. It lives in the desert. It can go for many days without drinking.

canary
A **canary** is a small bird that sings. **Canaries** are often kept as pets in cages.

cat
A **cat** has soft fur and sharp claws. **Cats** are good pets.

animals, living creatures

caterpillar
A **caterpillar** turns into a butterfly or a moth.

centipede
A **centipede** has many legs. It can run very fast.

chaffinch
A **chaffinch** is a small bird. It lives in bushes and trees.

chickens
Chickens often live on a farm.

chimpanzee
A **chimpanzee** is a small ape. It lives in trees.

cockerel
The **cockerel** is a male chicken. It crows early in the morning.

cow
We get milk from a **cow**. **Cows** eat grass.

crab
A **crab** is a sea animal. It has a hard shell and strong claws.

crocodile
The **crocodile** is a large reptile. It lives in or near rivers in hot lands. It has scaly skin.

crow
A **crow** is a big bird. It is black and has a loud cry.

animals, living creatures

cub
A young animal is sometimes called a **cub**. **Cubs** like to play.

daddy long legs
A **daddy long legs** is an insect that flies. It has very long legs.

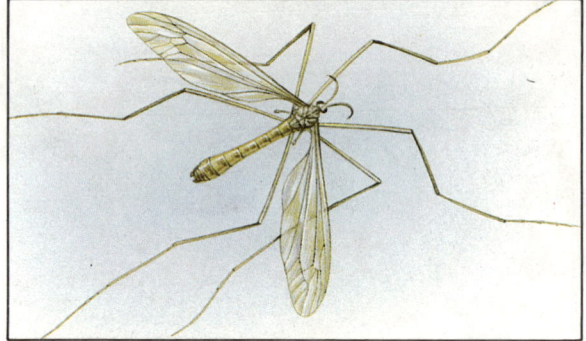

deer
A **deer** is a shy animal. It can run very fast.

dinosaur
Dinosaurs were huge reptiles that lived many, many years ago. There were several kinds of **dinosaurs**. There are no **dinosaurs** alive now.

dog
A **dog** barks and wags its tail. There are many different kinds of **dogs**.

dolphin
A **dolphin** lives in the sea. **Dolphins** come to the surface to breathe air. They can learn to do tricks.

donkey
A **donkey** looks like a small horse. It has long ears.

dormouse
A **dormouse** looks like a mouse with a bushy tail. It sleeps in the winter.

dragonfly
A **dragonfly** is a flying insect. It has four wings that you can see through.

duck
A **duck** is a bird that can fly and swim.

animals, living creatures

eagle
An **eagle** is a big, strong bird. It builds its nest in high places.

earwig
An **earwig** is a small insect.

elephant
An **elephant** has a trunk and tusks. It is the largest land animal.

emu
An **emu** is a large bird from Australia. It cannot fly but it runs very fast.

fish
Fish live in water. They use their fins and tail for swimming. There are many different kinds of **fish**.

fly
A **fly** is an insect with wings. **Flies** like the warm weather.

foal
A **foal** is a young horse.

fox
A **fox** is a wild animal. It sleeps in the day and looks for food at night.

frog
A **frog** hops on land and swims in water.

gerbil
A **gerbil** looks like a small mouse. **Gerbils** are good pets.

animals, living creatures

giraffe
A **giraffe** has a very long neck and long legs.

goat
We can get milk from a **goat**. Some **goats** have horns and a beard.

goldfish
A **goldfish** is a small orange fish. **Goldfish** are often kept in glass bowls or tanks.

goose
A **goose** has webbed feet. **Geese** can fly and swim.

gorilla
The **gorilla** is a large, strong animal. It lives in Africa.

grasshopper
A **grasshopper** is a small insect. **Grasshoppers** can jump a long way.

grass snake
The **grass snake** hides in long grass. It sleeps in the winter.

guinea pig
A **guinea pig** is a small, furry animal with no tail. **Guinea pigs** make good pets.

guppy
A **guppy** is a very small fish. **Guppies** can be kept in a fish tank.

hamster
A **hamster** can keep food in its cheeks. **Hamsters** are often kept as pets.

animals, living creatures

hare
A **hare** looks like a large rabbit. It can run very fast.

hedgehog
A **hedgehog** has prickles on its back. It can roll into a ball.

hen
A **hen** lays eggs. **Hens** often live in farmyards.

heron
A **heron** is a bird with long legs. It eats fish.

herring
A **herring** is a small fish that lives in the sea.

hippopotamus
A **hippopotamus** is a very large animal. It has thick skin and lives in or near water.

horse
You can ride a **horse**. **Horses** like hay to eat.

insect
An **insect** is a small creature with six legs. Many **insects** fly.

jay
A **jay** is a noisy bird. It has bright feathers.

kangaroo
A **kangaroo** jumps on its hind legs. Baby **kangaroos** are carried in their mother's pouch.

animals, living creatures

kid
A **kid** is a baby goat.

kingfisher
A **kingfisher** is a small bird with bright feathers. It lives near water and catches fish.

kitten
A **kitten** is a baby cat. **Kittens** are very playful.

koala bear
A **koala bear** is a small, furry animal from Australia. It lives in trees.

ladybird
A **ladybird** is an insect that flies. Most **ladybirds** are red with black spots.

lamb
A **lamb** is a baby sheep.
Lambs are born in spring.

leopard
A **leopard** is a big, wild cat. It has spots.

lion
A **lion** is a large, fierce animal. It is found in Africa.

lizard
A **lizard** has a long tail and short legs. **Lizards** eat insects.

lobster
A **lobster** lives in the sea. It has two large claws.

animals, living creatures

animals, living creatures

mole
A **mole** is a little, furry animal that lives underground.

monkey
A **monkey** is a small animal with a long tail. **Monkeys** are good at climbing trees.

mosquito
A **mosquito** is a flying insect. It can sting us. Some **mosquitoes** carry diseases.

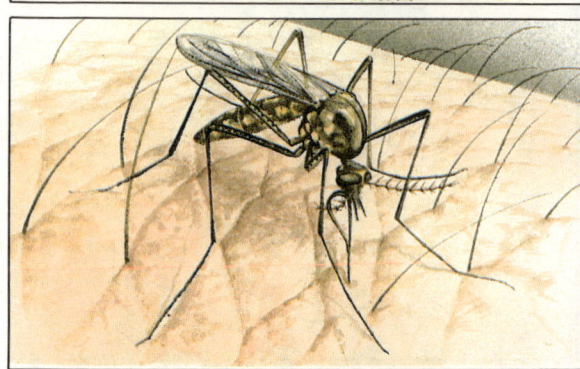

moth
A **moth** looks like a butterfly. **Moths** fly at night.

mouse
A **mouse** is a small animal with a long tail. **Mice** have sharp teeth.

newt
A **newt** looks like a small lizard. It can live in or out of water.

octopus
An **octopus** is a sea animal. It has eight arms.

otter
An **otter** lives near water. It is a good swimmer and eats fish.

owl
An **owl** is a bird with large eyes. It can see well in the dark.

panda
A **panda** looks like a bear. **Pandas** come from China.

animals, living creatures

parrot
A **parrot** is a large bird. Some **parrots** can learn to talk by copying.

peacock
The **peacock** is a bird with beautiful tail feathers. It spreads its tail like a fan.

penguin
A **penguin** is a bird which can swim but cannot fly. **Penguins** eat fish.

pig
A **pig** is a farm animal. **Pigs** have curly tails.

pigeon
A **pigeon** is a bird. Some **pigeons** can be kept as pets.

piglet
A **piglet** is a baby pig.

polar bear
The **polar bear** is a large, white animal. It lives near the North Pole.

pony
A **pony** is a small horse.

porcupine
A **porcupine** is covered with sharp quills.

prawn
A **prawn** is a small sea animal. It is good to eat.

puppy
A **puppy** is a young dog. **Puppies** like to play.

rabbit
A wild **rabbit** lives in a burrow. Pet **rabbits** are kept in a hutch.

rat
A **rat** has sharp teeth and a long tail. It is like a large mouse.

reindeer
A **reindeer** has large antlers. **Reindeer** live in the cold lands of the north.

rhinoceros
A **rhinoceros** is a large and heavy animal. It has one or two long horns on its nose.

robin
The **robin** is a garden bird. It has a red breast.

rook
The **rook** is a large, black bird. **Rooks** nest together in high trees.

seagull
The **seagull** is a bird that lives near the sea. **Seagulls** have a loud call. They eat fish.

seahorse
The **seahorse** is a small sea animal with a curly tail.

seal
A **seal** swims in the sea and eats fish. **Seals** live on the land and in the water.

animals, living creatures

shark
The **shark** is a very large fish. It has huge, sharp teeth.

sheep
A **sheep** has a thick coat of wool.

snail
A **snail** is a small creature often found in gardens. It has a shell on its back. **Snails** move very slowly.

snake
A **snake** is long and thin. It has no legs.

sparrow
A **sparrow** is a small bird. **Sparrows** eat insects and seeds.

spider
A **spider** has eight long legs. Many **spiders** spin a web to catch insects.

squirrel
A **squirrel** has a big, bushy tail. It lives in trees and eats nuts.

starfish
A **starfish** is a sea animal shaped like a star.

stegosaurus
A **stegosaurus** was a dinosaur. It was a plant eater.

stickleback
The **stickleback** is a small fish. It lives in rivers and ponds.

animals, living creatures

stoat
A **stoat** is a small, furry animal. It eats other animals.

swallow
The **swallow** is a bird with a forked tail. It flies to warm lands when the weather is cold.

swan
A **swan** is a bird that can fly and swim. **Swans** always live near water.

thrush
The **thrush** is a song bird. It has a speckled breast.

tiger
The **tiger** is a fierce animal like a large cat. Its fur is striped.

toad
A **toad** looks like a large frog. It has a rough skin and lives mainly on land.

tortoise
The tortoise moves slowly. It has a thick, hard shell.

turkey
A **turkey** is a large bird. It is seen in farmyards.

turtle
A **turtle** can swim. It has a hard shell. **Turtles** lay eggs on land.

tyrannosaurus rex
A **tyrannosaurus rex** was the tallest dinosaur. It was a meat eater.

animals, living creatures

animals, living creatures

walrus
The **walrus** is a sea animal. It looks like a large seal. It has two tusks.

wasp
A **wasp** is an insect that flies. It can sting.

whale
The **whale** is a large sea animal. It comes to the surface of the sea to breathe air.

wildcat
The **wildcat** is a fierce animal. It has sharp claws.

wolf
A **wolf** is a wild animal like a large dog. It howls at night.

woodlouse
The **woodlouse** is a small creature. You can find **woodlice** under a stone or under leaves.

woodpecker
The **woodpecker** has a strong beak. It pecks holes in trees to catch insects.

worm
A **worm** is small and thin. It has no legs. Many **worms** live in the ground.

zebra
A **zebra** has stripes. It comes from Africa.

animals, living creatures

my body

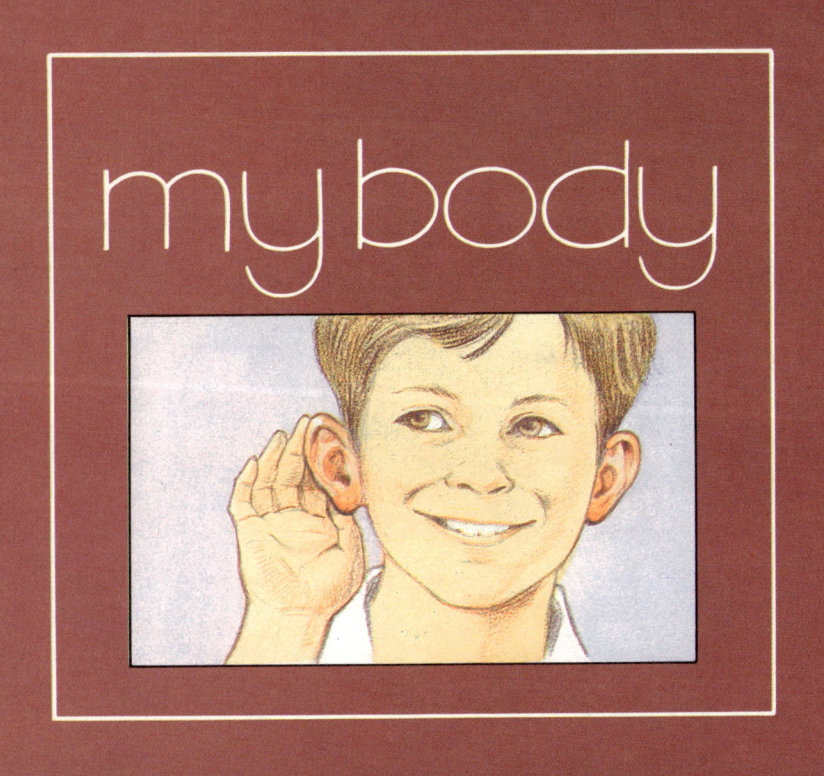

ankle
Your **ankle** is the joint between your foot and your leg.

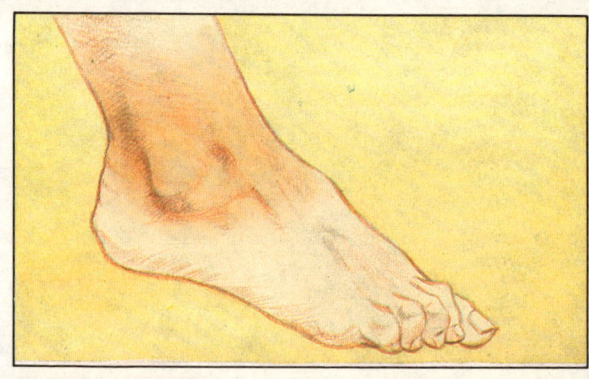

arm
Your **arm** is between your shoulder and your hand.

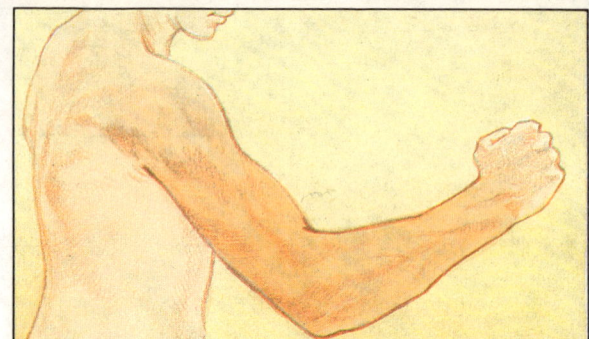

blood
Blood is the red liquid inside you. **Blood** takes food and air round your body.

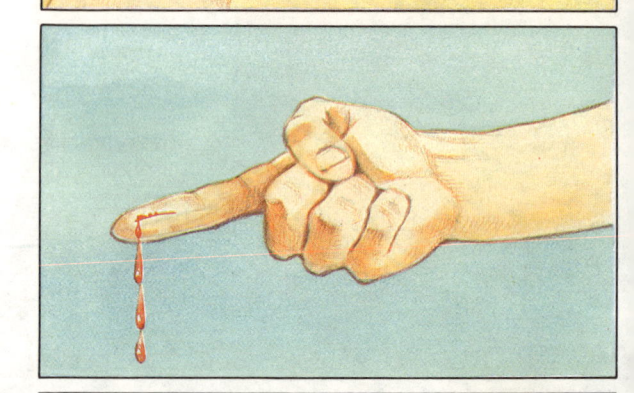

body
The **body** is all the parts of a person or animal.

bones
Bones support your body. They are hard.

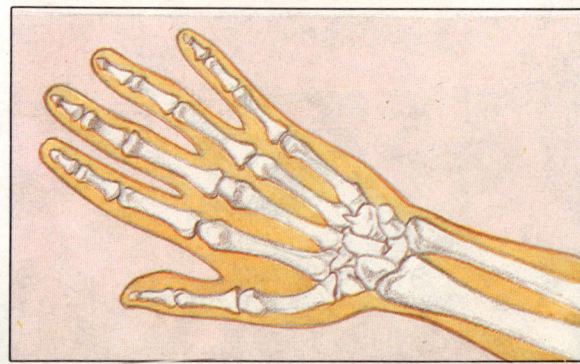

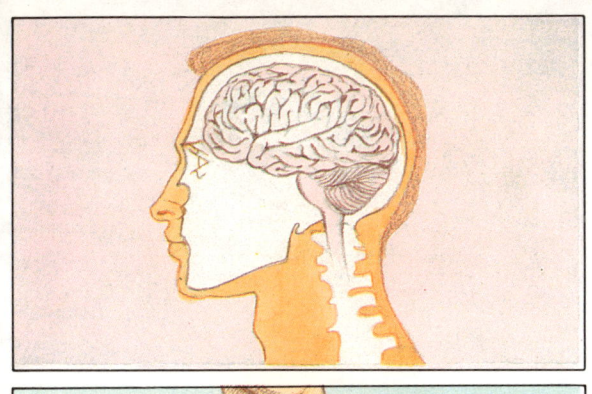

brain
Your **brain** is inside your head. It controls your body.

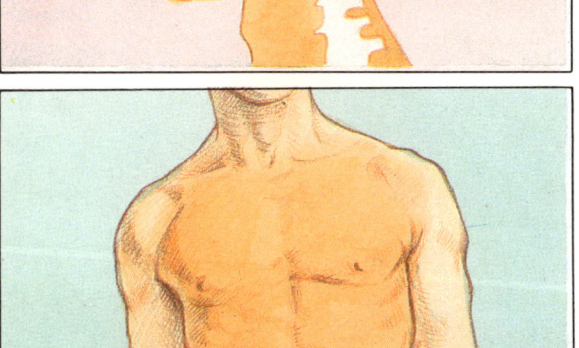

chest
Your **chest** is between your neck and your waist. It contains your lungs.

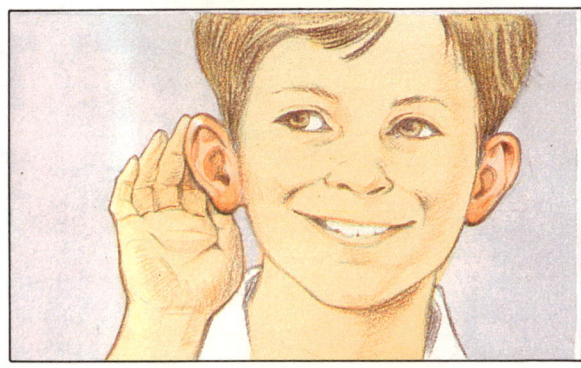

ears
You hear with your **ears**.

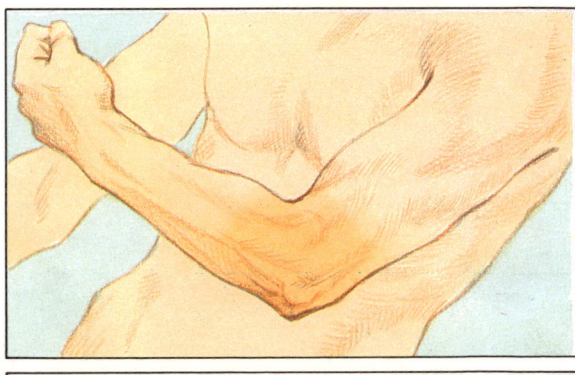

elbow
You can bend your arm at your **elbow**. It is between your shoulder and your wrist.

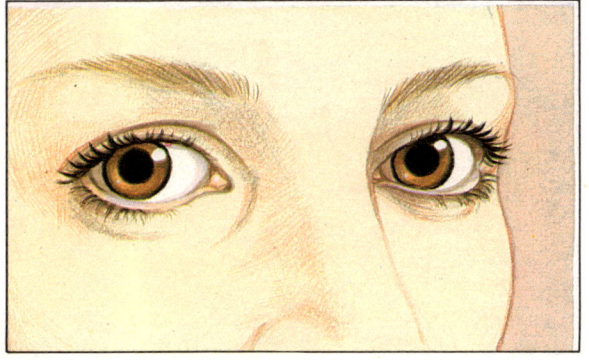

eyes
You see with your **eyes**.

my body

my body

face
Your **face** is at the front of your head.

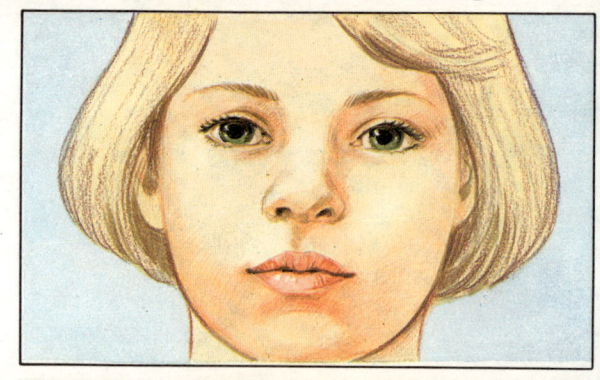

feet
Your **feet** are at the end of your legs. You walk on your **feet**.

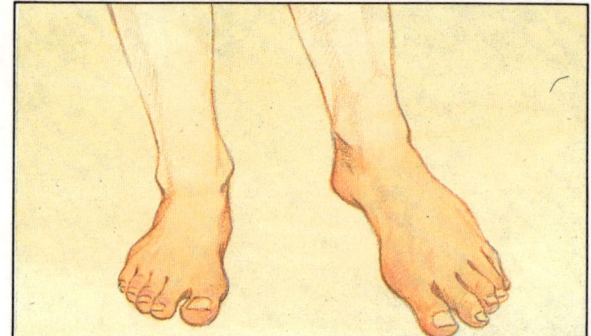

fingers
Fingers are part of your hand. You use your **fingers** to hold things.

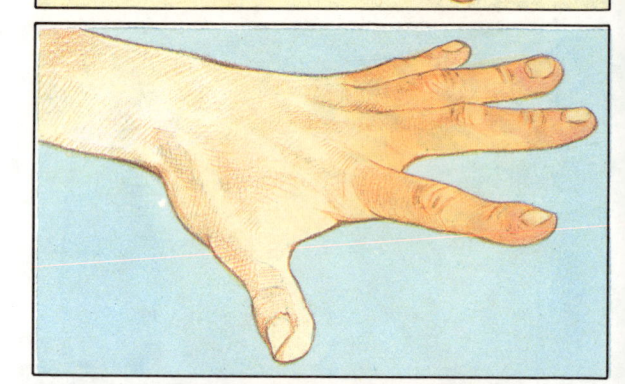

hair
Hair grows on the top of your head. We brush our **hair** to keep it tidy.

hand
You have four fingers and one thumb on each **hand**. Your **hands** are at the end of your arms.

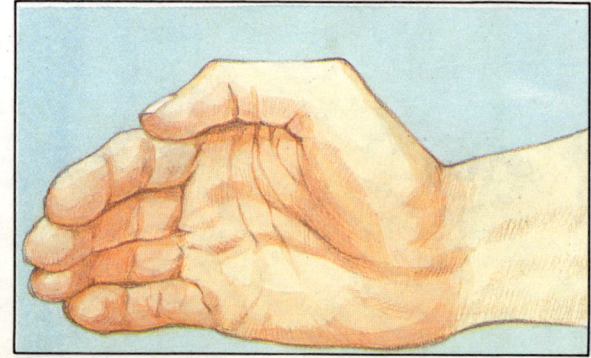

head
Your **head** is above your neck.

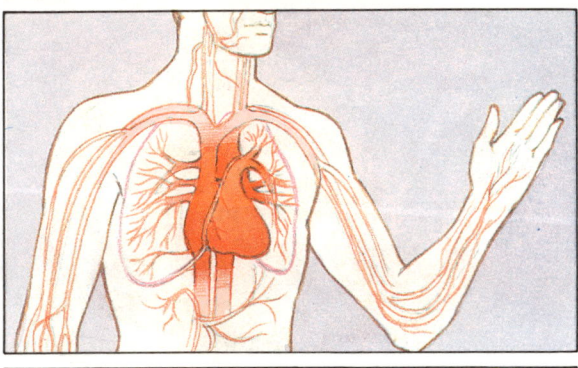

heart
Your **heart** sends the blood round your body.

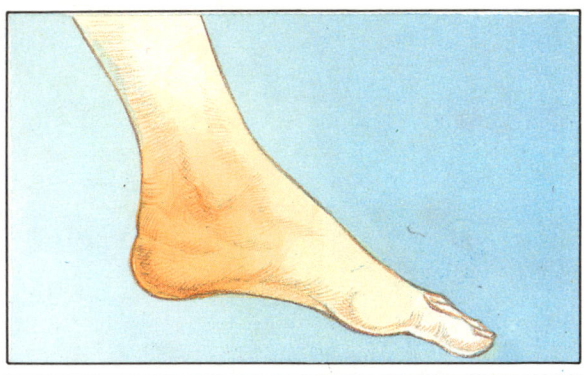

heel
Your **heel** is the back part of your foot.

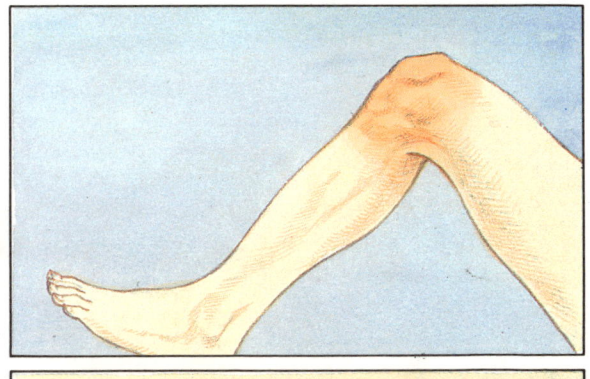

knee
Your **knee** is where you bend your leg.

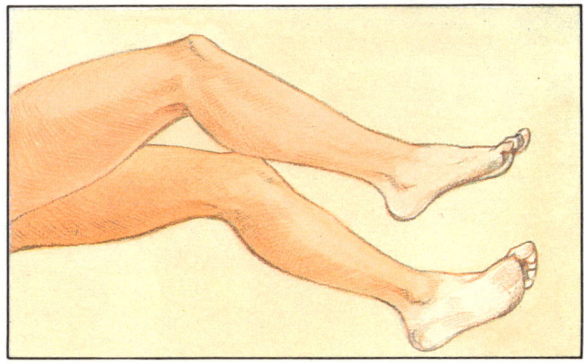

legs
You stand and move on your **legs**.

my body

47

my body

mouth
You put food into your **mouth** when you eat. You also talk through your **mouth**.

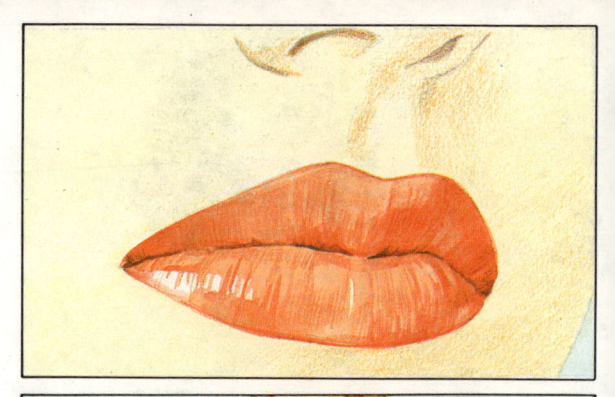

muscles
Muscles help your body to move.

nail
We have a **nail** on each finger and toe. We cut **nails** when they grow long.

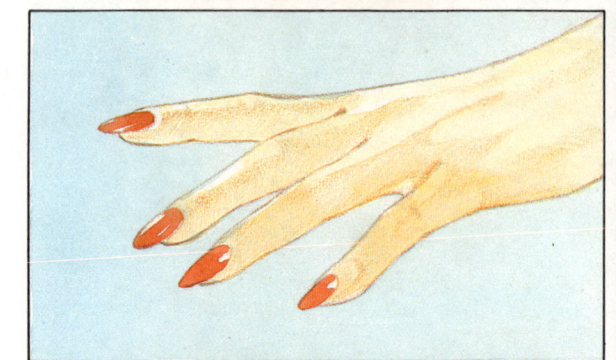

neck
Your **neck** is between your head and your shoulders.

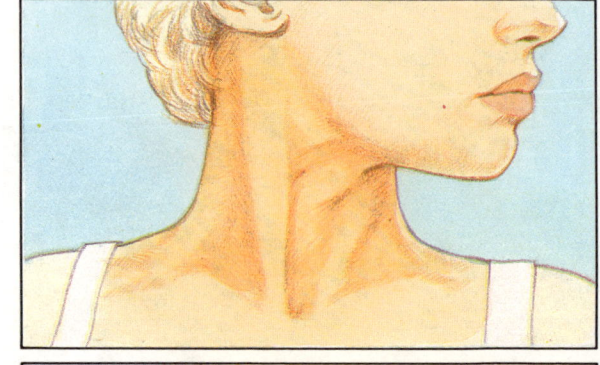

nose
You use your **nose** to smell and to breathe.

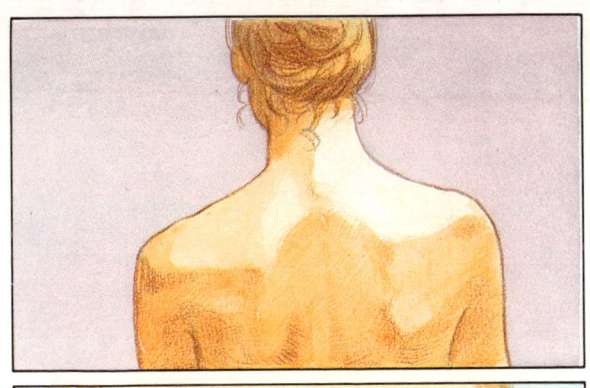

shoulders
Your **shoulders** are between your neck and your arms.

skin
Skin is the covering of your body.

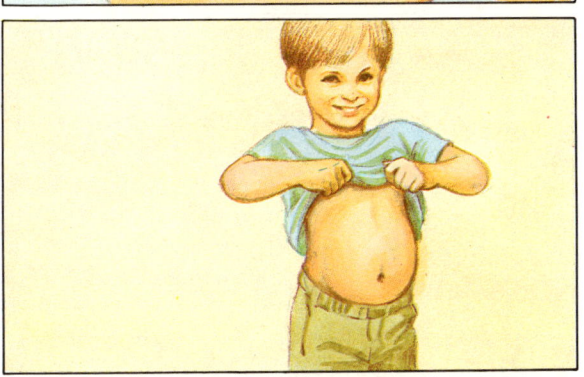

stomach
Food goes into your **stomach**. Your **stomach** uses it to give you energy.

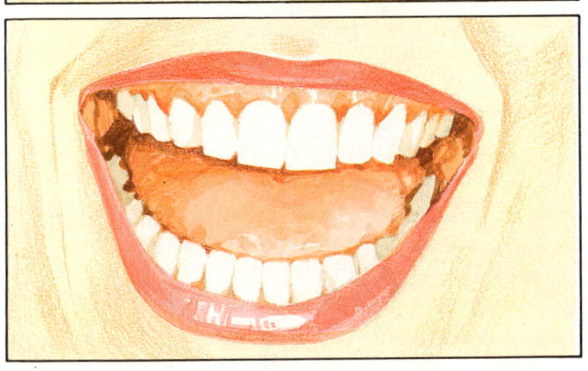

teeth
Teeth are in your mouth. You bite and chew with your **teeth**.

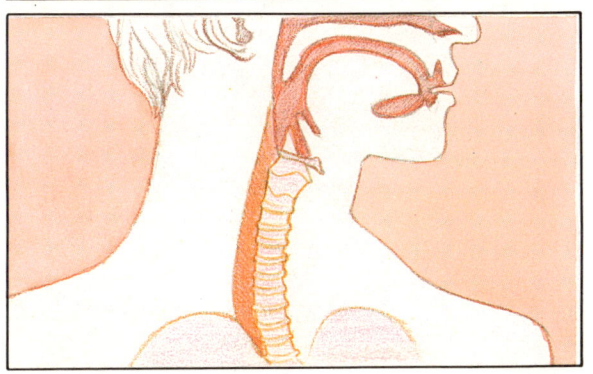

throat
Your **throat** takes air and food from your mouth to the inside of your body.

my body

49

my body

thumb
You have a **thumb** on each hand.

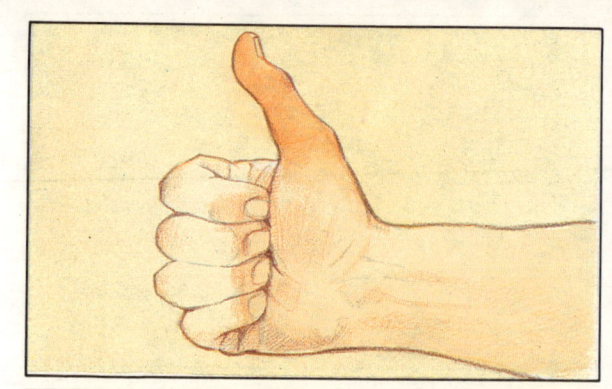

toes
You have five **toes** on each foot.

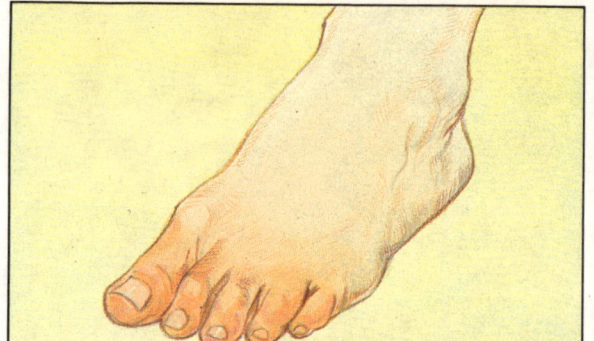

waist
Your **waist** is the middle of your body. You can wear a belt round your **waist**.

wrist
Your **wrist** is between your hand and arm. You can wear a watch on your **wrist**.

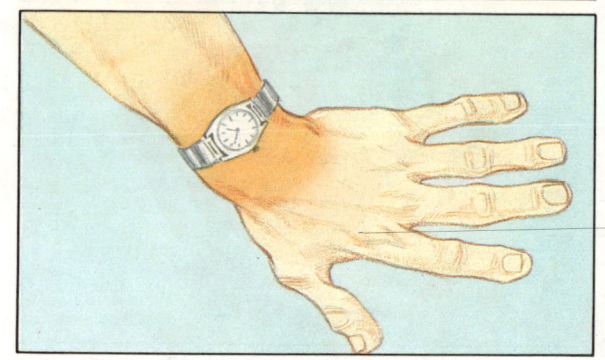

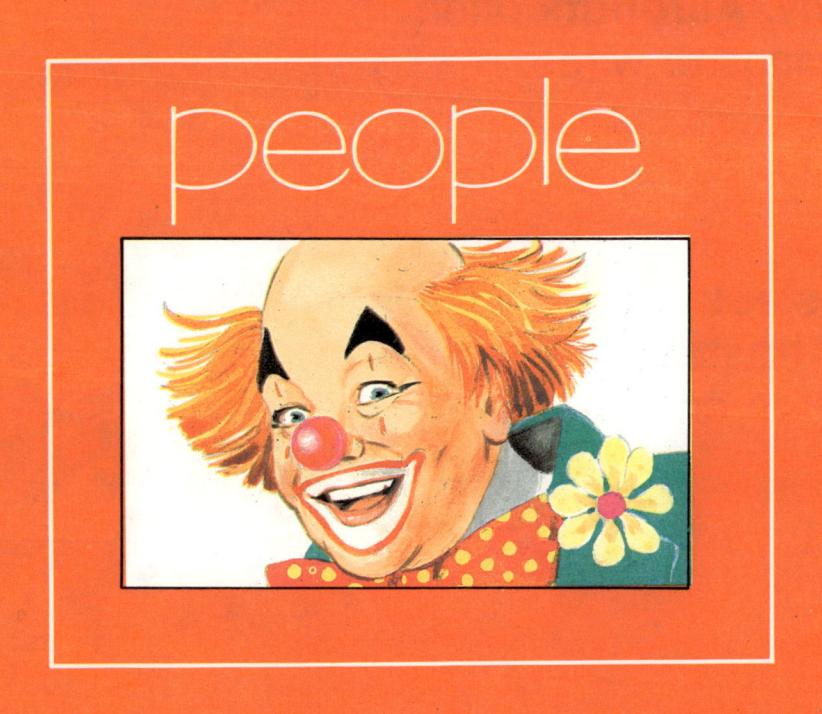

people

people

acrobat
An **acrobat** does tricks with his body. **Acrobats** often use swings or wires.

air hostess
An **air hostess** looks after people on an aeroplane.

artist
An **artist** paints pictures.

astronaut
An **astronaut** travels in space in a capsule or a space shuttle.

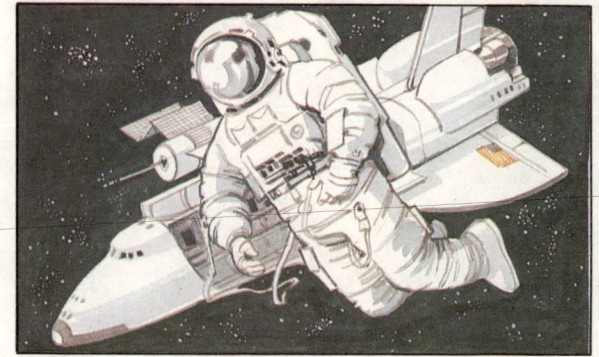

athlete
An **athlete** is very good at sport.

aunt
An **aunt** is the sister of one of your parents or the wife of your uncle.

baby
A **baby** is a very young child.

baker
A **baker** makes bread, cakes and pies.

boy
A **boy** grows up to be a man.

bride
A **bride** is a woman who is getting married.

people

bridegroom
A **bridegroom** is a man who is getting married.

brother
A boy is a **brother** to the other children of his parents.

child
A **child** is a young girl or boy.

clown
A **clown** makes people laugh.

cook
A **cook** gets meals ready.

cousin
A **cousin** is a child of your aunt or uncle.

cowboy
A **cowboy** works on a ranch and rides a horse.

crowd
A large number of people is called a **crowd**.

dad
Dad is a short name for father.

daughter
A **daughter** is a girl child.

people

dentist
A **dentist** looks after teeth.

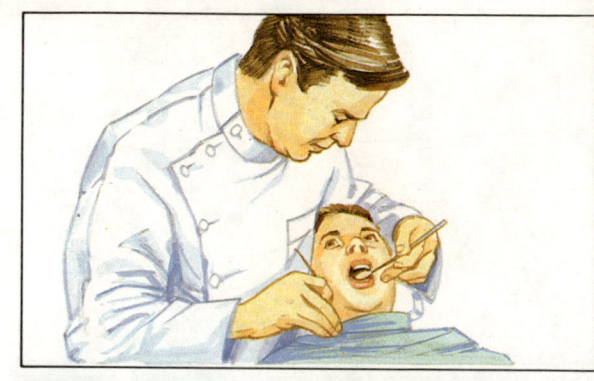

diver
A **diver** can swim under water.

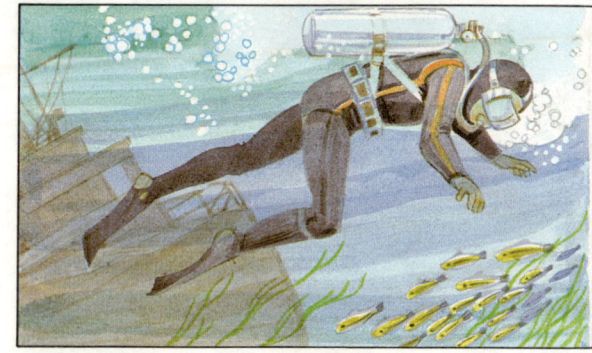

doctor
A **doctor** decides how to help people get better when they are ill.

driver
A **driver** steers a bus, car, or lorry.

dustman
A **dustman** carries away our rubbish. He empties it into his lorry.

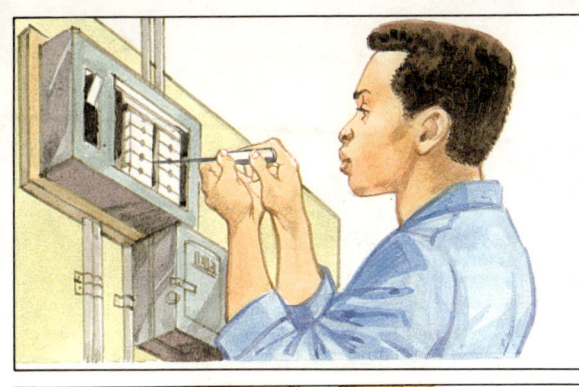

electrician
An **electrician** mends electrical things.

family
A mum, a dad and their children are a **family**. Grandparents, aunts, uncles and cousins also belong to their **family**.

farmer
A **farmer** lives and works on a farm.

father
Father is another name for dad.

fireman
A **fireman** puts out fires. He comes in a fire engine.

people

people

footballer
A **footballer** plays football for a team.

girl
A **girl** grows up to be a woman.

grandchild
You are a **grandchild** of your grandmother and grandfather.

grandfather
Your **grandfather** is the father of your mother or father.

grandmother
Your **grandmother** is the mother of your mother or father.

hairdresser
A **hairdresser** looks after people's hair.

husband
When two people get married the man is called the **husband**.

lady
Lady is another word for woman.

librarian
A **librarian** works in a library. **Librarians** look after the books.

man
A boy grows up to be a man.

people

59

people

mechanic
A **mechanic** can repair machines.

miner
A **miner** works underground.

mother
Mother is another word for mum.

neighbour
A **neighbour** is someone who lives near you.

nephew
A **nephew** is the son of a brother or sister.

niece
A **niece** is the daughter of a brother or sister.

nurse
A **nurse** takes care of sick people.

painter
A **painter** paints the inside and outside of houses. An artist who paints pictures is also called a **painter**.

parents
Mum and Dad are the **parents** of their children.

people
Girls, boys, babies, men and women are **people**.

people

61

people

person
A **person** is any girl, boy, woman or man.

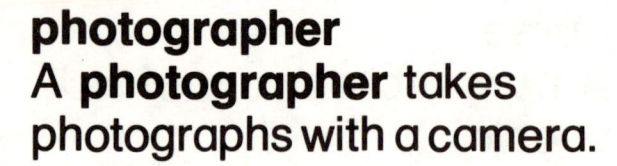

photographer
A **photographer** takes photographs with a camera.

pilot
A **pilot** flies an aeroplane.

plumber
A **plumber** mends leaking water pipes and broken taps.

policeman
A **policeman** is a man who belongs to the police. The police catch people who break the law.

policewoman
A **policewoman** is a woman who belongs to the police. **Policewomen** and policemen work together.

postman
A **postman** brings letters and parcels to houses.

queue
When a line of people have to wait, they make a **queue**.

relatives
My aunt and uncle are two of my **relatives**. They are part of my family.

sailor
A **sailor** works on a ship.

people

shepherd
A **shepherd** looks after sheep.

shopkeeper
A **shopkeeper** looks after a shop.

sister
A girl is a **sister** to the other children of her parents.

soldier
A **soldier** is in the army.

son
A **son** is a boy child.

star
A **star** is someone famous in television or films.

teacher
A **teacher** helps children to learn.

twin
Twins are born at the same time to one mother.

typist
A **typist** types letters to make them easier to read.

uncle
An **uncle** is the brother of one of your parents or the husband of your aunt.

people

vet
A **vet** looks after sick animals.

waiter
A **waiter** is a man who serves food.

waitress
A **waitress** is a woman who serves food.

wife
When two people get married, the woman is called a **wife**.

woman
A girl grows up to be a **woman**.

food and drink

food and drink

bacon
Bacon comes from a pig. We buy slices of **bacon**.

beef
Beef is the meat that comes from cows.

biscuit
A **biscuit** is made with flour, sugar and fat. **Biscuits** are baked in an oven.

bread
Bread is made from flour, water and yeast. Yeast makes the **bread** rise before it goes into the oven.

butter
Butter is made from cream. You put **butter** on bread and toast.

cake
A **cake** is made from flour, butter, eggs and sugar. **Cakes** are baked in an oven.

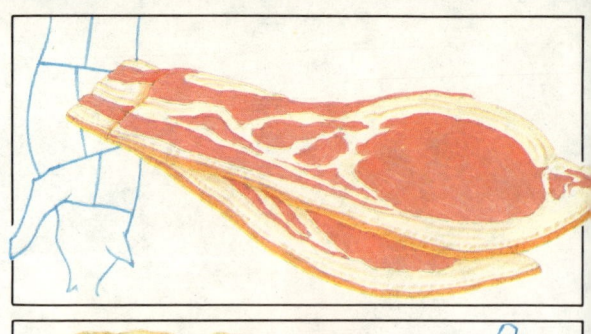

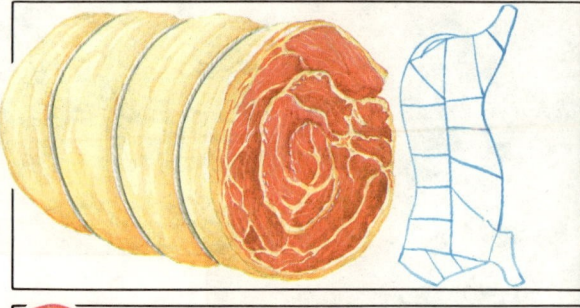

food and drink

cheese
Cheese is made from milk. There are many kinds of **cheese**.

chip
A **chip** is a piece of fried potato. **Chips** are fried in fat.

chocolate
Chocolate is made from cocoa beans, milk and sugar.

coffee
Coffee is a hot drink. It is made from **coffee** beans or **coffee** powder.

cone
We can put ice cream inside a **cone**. It tastes like a biscuit.

cornflakes
Cornflakes are made from sweetcorn or maize. We eat **cornflakes** for breakfast.

food and drink

custard
Custard is a sauce we can put on puddings. It is made from eggs, milk, flour and sugar.

egg
An **egg** comes from a hen. You can cook **eggs** in several ways. They go into cakes and pancakes.

fish finger
A **fish finger** is a thin piece of fish coated in egg and breadcrumbs.

hamburger
A **hamburger** is made of fried chopped meat. It often comes in a bun.

honey
Honey is very sweet. Bees make **honey**.

hot dog
A **hot dog** is a hot sausage inside a long roll.

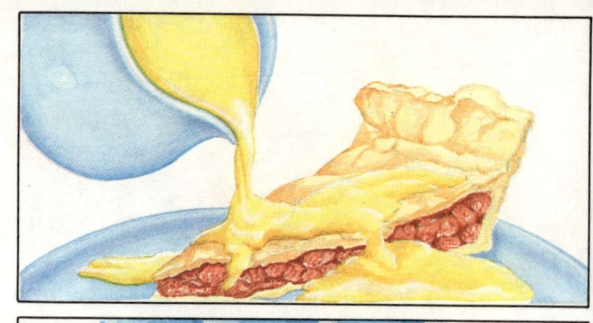

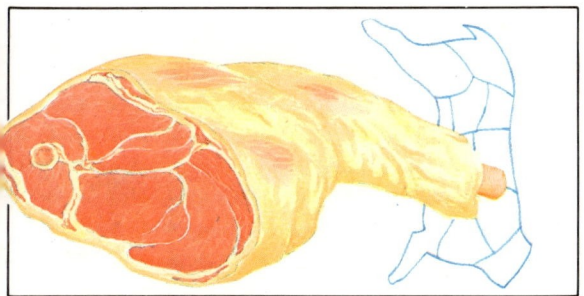

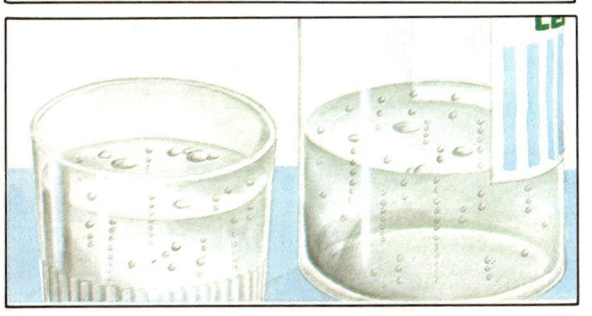

ice-cream
Ice-cream is cold and sweet. It is frozen cream and sugar.

jam
Jam is made from fruit and sugar. There are many kinds of **jam**.

jelly
A **jelly** sets when it is cold. It tastes fruity and it wobbles.

lamb
Lamb is meat that comes from young sheep.

lemonade
Lemonade is made from lemon juice, sugar and water. Sometimes it is fizzy.

lollipop
A **lollipop** is a sweet on a stick.

food and drink

food and drink

marmalade
Marmalade is a jam made of oranges or lemons. We eat it for breakfast.

meat
Meat comes from animals. There are many kinds of **meat**.

milk
Milk comes from cows. We drink **milk**.

milk shake
A **milk shake** is milk and fruit juice mixed together.

orange juice
Orange juice is squeezed from oranges.

pancake
A **pancake** is made from flour, eggs and milk. **Pancakes** are cooked in a frying pan. We toss them to turn them over.

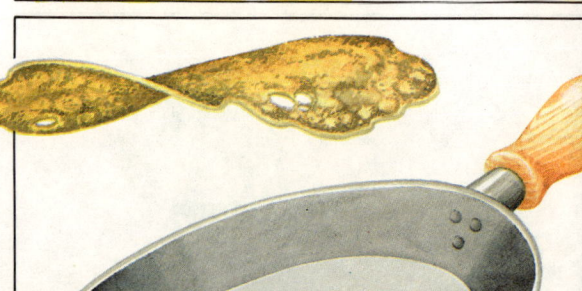

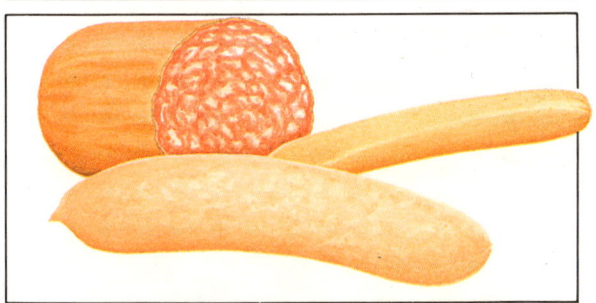

pie
A **pie** is pastry over meat or fruit. **Pies** are baked in an oven.

pork
Pork is the meat that comes from pigs.

pudding
A **pudding** is eaten at the end of a meal. **Puddings** are sweet.

sandwich
A **sandwich** is two pieces of bread with some filling in between them.

sausage
A **sausage** is minced meat put inside a skin.

sausage roll
A **sausage roll** is sausage meat cooked in pastry.

food and drink

food and drink

soup
Soup is made from meat or vegetables and wate**r**. We often start a meal with **soup**.

sweet
A **sweet** is made of sugar. Too many **sweets** harm your teeth.

tea
You make **tea** by pouring boiling water on **tea** leaves. Some people add milk and sugar to their **tea**.

toast
Toast is bread that is grilled until it is brown.

water
You can drink **water**. You can wash with **water**.

yoghurt
Yoghurt is made from milk. It is thick and a little sour.

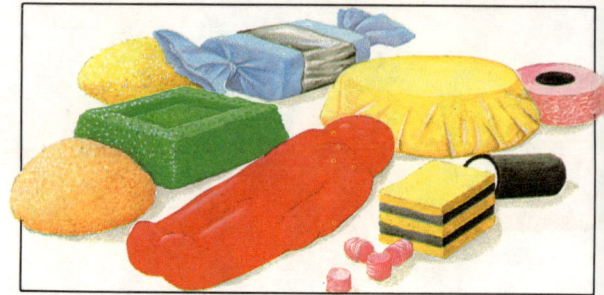

apple
An **apple** is a hard, round fruit. **Apples** grow on trees.

banana
A **banana** is a sweet, yellow fruit. It has a thick skin.

cherry
A **cherry** is a small, round fruit. It has a stone in the middle.

grape
A **grape** is a small, round fruit. **Grapes** grow in bunches.

grapefruit
A **grapefruit** is like a large orange. It has a yellow skin and a sour taste.

lemon
A **lemon** is a sour, yellow fruit.

melon
A **melon** is a large, sweet fruit with lots of juice.

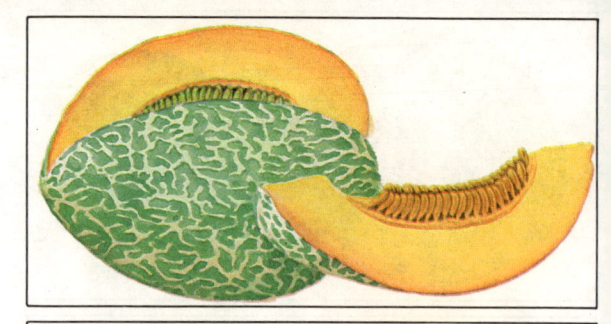

orange
An **orange** is a round, sweet fruit. It is full of juice.

peach
A **peach** is a sweet fruit. It has a soft, furry skin and a large stone in the middle.

pear
A **pear** is a very juicy fruit. It is rounded at one end and pointed at the other.

pineapple
A **pineapple** is a large, sweet fruit. It has a spiky skin.

plum
A **plum** is a small, soft fruit. **Plums** grow on trees.

raspberry
A **raspberry** is a sweet, soft berry. **Raspberries** grow on bushes.

rhubarb
Rhubarb has a long stalk with a large, green leaf. You can only eat the stalk.

strawberry
A **strawberry** is a small, sweet berry. It has seeds on the outside.

tangerine
A **tangerine** looks like a small orange. It is sweet and easy to peel.

tomato
A **tomato** is a soft fruit with a red skin.

fruit

vegetables

bean
A **bean** is a large seed. It grows in a pod. You can eat the pod of some **beans**.

beetroot
A **beetroot** is a dark red vegetable. It grows under the ground.

broccoli
Broccoli is a green vegetable. You can eat the stalk and the buds.

cabbage
A **cabbage** is a large, round vegetable. It has many thick leaves.

carrot
A **carrot** is an orange vegetable. It grows under the ground.

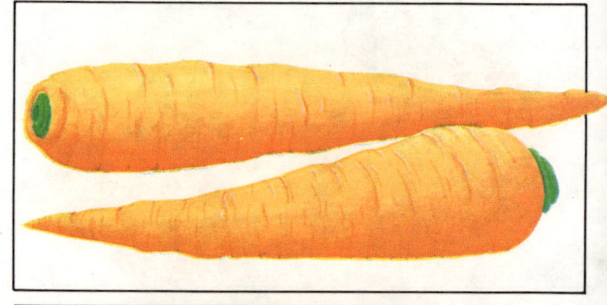

cauliflower
The **cauliflower** is a large, white vegetable.

vegetables

celery
Celery has long, crunchy stalks.

cucumber
A **cucumber** is long and green. We eat it in salad.

leek
A **leek** is a long, white and green vegetable. It tastes like an onion.

marrow
A **marrow** is like a large cucumber. It has a thick skin.

mushroom
A **mushroom** looks like a tiny umbrella.

onion
An **onion** has a strong taste and smell.

vegetables

pea
A **pea** is a round seed. It grows in a pod.

pepper
A **pepper** is a red, green or yellow vegetable.

potato
A **potato** has a brown skin. **Potatoes** grow under the ground.

sprout
A **sprout** looks like a very small cabbage.

sweetcorn
Sweetcorn is a yellow seed. It grows on a cob.

turnip
A **turnip** is a white or yellow vegetable. It grows under the ground.

things we wear

things we wear

anorak
An **anorak** is a jacket with a zip and hood. It keeps us warm and dry.

apron
An **apron** keeps your clothes clean in the kitchen.

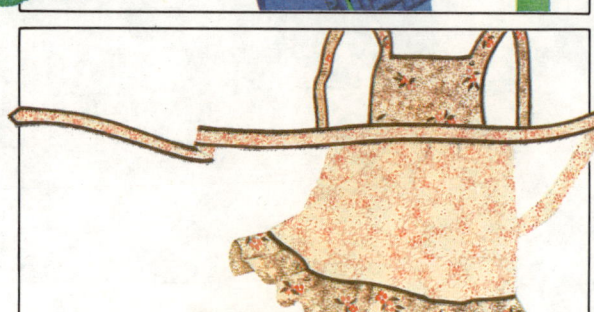

beads
Beads are worn round the neck.

belt
A **belt** is worn round the waist.

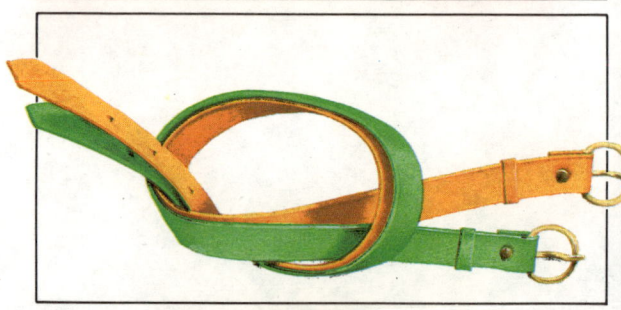

blouse
A **blouse** is worn with a skirt or trousers by women and girls.

boots
We wear **boots** on our feet to keep them warm.

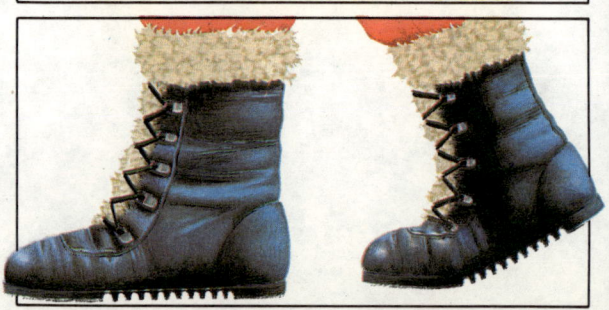

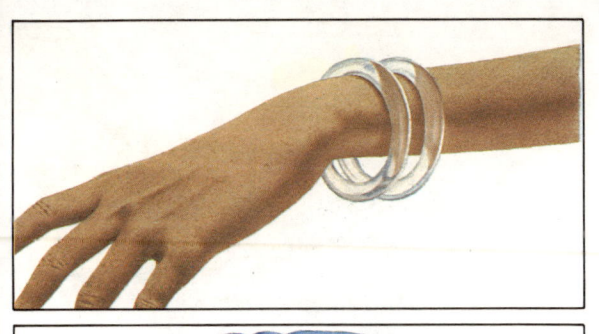

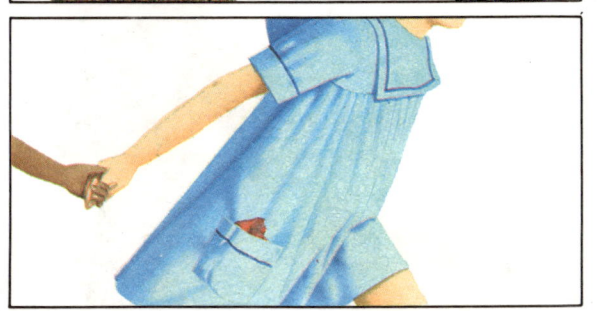

bracelet
We wear a **bracelet** on our wrist or ankle.

cap
A **cap** is worn on the head.

cardigan
A **cardigan** has buttons down the front and is worn over a shirt or dress.

coat
We wear a **coat** over our clothes when we go out.

dress
A **dress** is worn by a girl or woman.

dressing gown
A **dressing gown** is worn over pyjamas or a nightdress.

things we wear

things we wear

football boots
We wear **football boots** to play football.

gloves
We wear **gloves** on our hands to keep them warm.

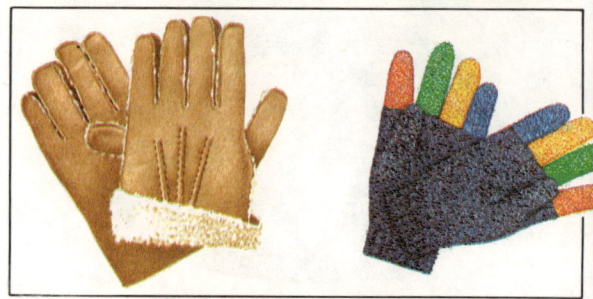

hairband
A **hairband** keeps your hair tidy.

hat
A **hat** is worn on the head.

jacket
A **jacket** is a short coat.

jeans
Jeans are a kind of trousers.

things we wear

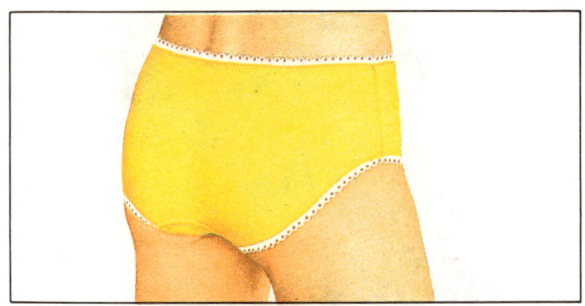

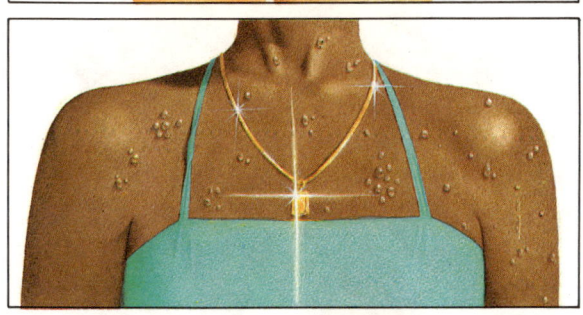

jumper
A **jumper** is knitted. It keeps you warm.

mittens
Mittens keep your hands warm. They have two parts, one for your thumb and one for the fingers.

nightdress
A **nightdress** is worn by girls and women in bed.

pants
We wear **pants** under skirts and trousers.

pendant
A **pendant** is worn round the neck.

pinafore dress
A **pinafore dress** is worn over a jumper or blouse.

things we wear

plimsolls
We wear **plimsolls** for PE or dancing.

pyjamas
Pyjamas are worn in bed.

raincoat
A **raincoat** helps to keep you dry on a rainy day.

ribbon
A **ribbon** is worn in the hair.

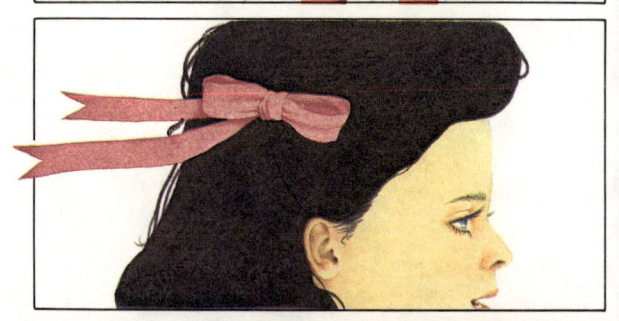

ring
We wear a **ring** on our finger. A wedding **ring** is often made of gold.

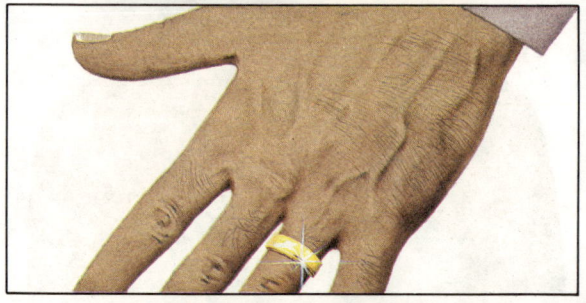

sandals
We wear **sandals** on our feet when it is warm. They help to keep our feet cool.

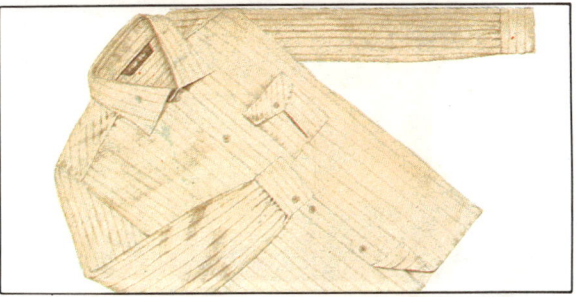

scarf
We wear a **scarf** round our neck to keep warm.

shirt
A **shirt** has a collar and sleeves. It has buttons down the front.

shoes
We wear **shoes** on our feet to keep them warm and dry.

skirt
Girls and women wear a **skirt** with a blouse or jumper.

socks
Socks keep your feet warm.

suit
A **suit** is a jacket with a matching skirt or trousers. Men and women wear suits.

things we wear

87

things we wear

sweater
A **sweater** is another name for a jumper.

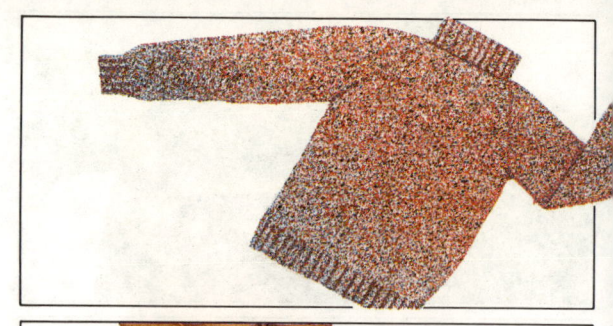

swimsuit
Women and girls wear a **swimsuit** when they swim.

tie
A **tie** is worn round the neck. It goes under a shirt collar.

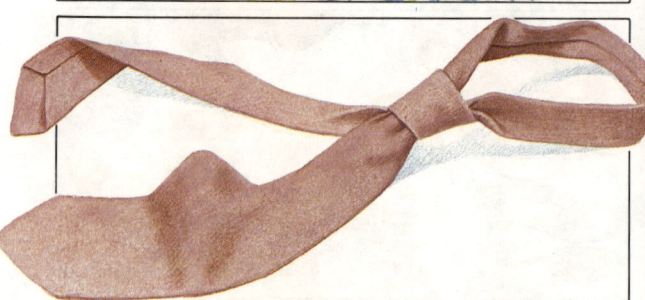

tights
Women and girls wear **tights** to keep their legs and feet warm.

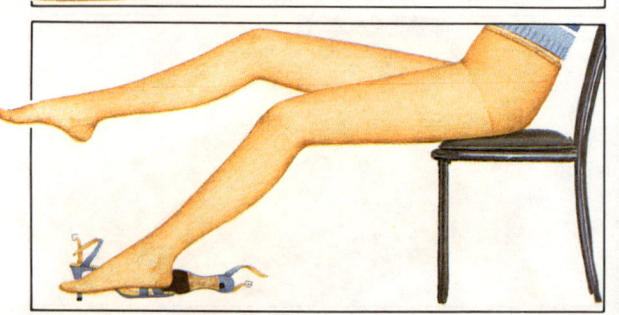

trainers
Trainers are shoes which are worn for running and other sports.

trousers
Trousers are worn to cover the legs.

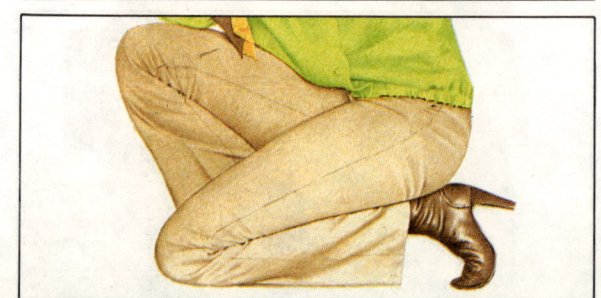

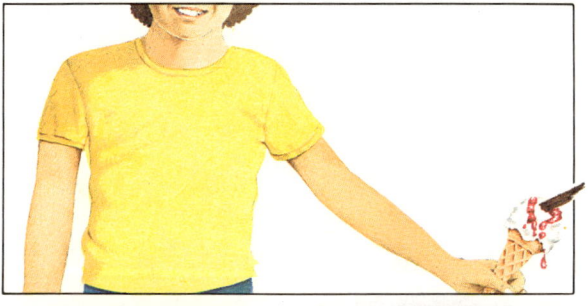

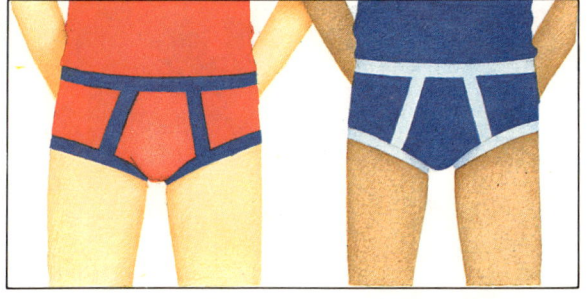

trunks
Boys and men wear **trunks** when they swim.

t-shirt
A **t-shirt** is a thin shirt with short sleeves.

underpants
Men and boys wear **underpants** under their trousers.

vest
A **vest** is worn under your shirt or blouse. It keeps you warm.

watch
A **watch** is a clock you can wear on your wrist.

wellingtons
Wellingtons are long rubber boots. They keep your feet dry in wet weather.

things we wear

at home

outside

aerial
An **aerial** is a metal rod. It helps make the television or radio work.

chimney
Smoke comes out through a **chimney** at the top of a house.

door
A **door** is the entrance to a house or a room.

drain
A **drain** carries waste water away from the house.

fence
Some houses have a wooden **fence** around the garden.

garage
A **garage** is where a car is kept.

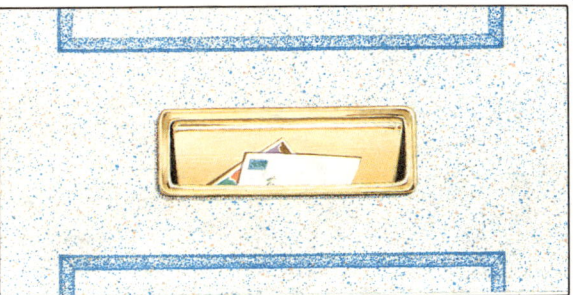

outside

gate
A **gate** is the opening in a fence.

letterbox
The postman delivers letters through a **letterbox**.

roof
A **roof** covers the top of a house.

step
Steps make it easy to climb up to the front door.

wall
A **wall** is usually made of bricks.

window
A **window** lets in light. You can open a **window** to let in air.

garage

bicycle
A **bicycle** has two wheels. Learn to ride a **bicycle** properly before going on a road.

car
A **car** uses petrol to move from one place to another.

caravan
A **caravan** is a house on wheels. We can stay in a **caravan** on holiday.

hammer
A **hammer** is a tool for hitting things. We can hit a nail with a **hammer**.

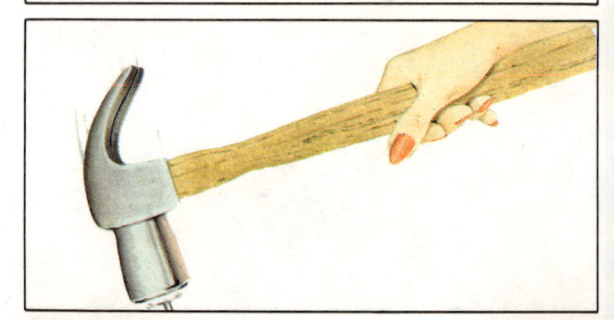

jack
We raise a car with a **jack**. It is used when we change a wheel.

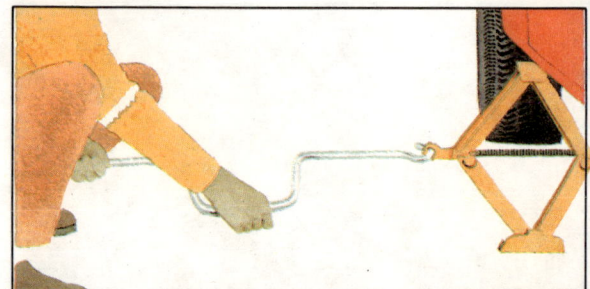

ladder
We climb a **ladder** to reach high places.

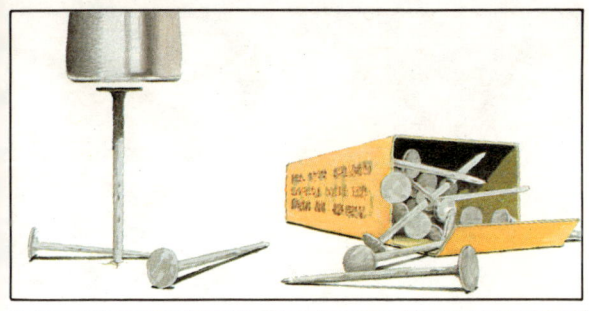

nails
Nails hold pieces of wood together.

saw
We can cut through wood with a **saw**.

screwdriver
A **screwdriver** turns a screw.

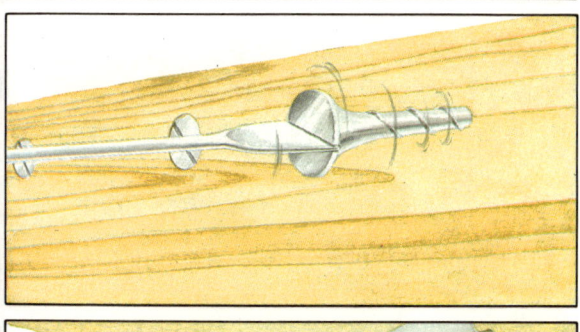

screws
Screws are used to hold two pieces of wood together.

spanner
We use a **spanner** to tighten up nuts.

tyres
Tyres go round wheels. They are full of air.

garage

garden

bird table
We put food on the **bird table**. Many birds come to feed on it.

fork
We use a **fork** to dig up weeds from the garden.

garden
Flowers, vegetables and trees grow in a **garden**.

greenhouse
A **greenhouse** is made of glass. It keeps flowers and plants warm inside.

hose
We use a **hose** to water plants and vegetables in a garden.

mower
A **mower** is used for cutting grass.

nesting box
Some birds build a nest in a **nesting box**.

rake
We use a **rake** to clear away leaves in the autumn.

shed
We keep our garden tools in the **shed**.

spade
We use a **spade** to dig a hole in the garden.

trowel
We use a **trowel** to dig a small hole.

wheelbarrow
A **wheelbarrow** is used for moving heavy or bulky things in the garden.

garden

kitchen

brush
We sweep up the dust with a **brush**.

bucket
You can carry water in a **bucket**.

chair
You sit on a **chair**.

coffee pot
A **coffee pot** holds coffee.

cooker
We use a **cooker** to cook food. It uses gas or electricity.

cup
We drink hot drinks from a **cup**.

kitchen

cupboard
We keep cups, plates and pans in a **cupboard**.

fork
We use a **fork** to lift food from a plate to our mouth.

freezer
We keep frozen food in a **freezer**. It keeps it fresh for a long time.

fridge
Food is kept in a **fridge** for a short time. The food keeps cold and fresh.

glass
We drink cold drinks from a **glass**.

iron
A hot **iron** makes clothes smooth.

kitchen

ironing board
We iron clothes on an **ironing board**.

jug
We can pour milk from a **jug**.

kettle
A **kettle** is used for boiling water.

knife
We use a **knife** to cut food.

mixer
We use a **mixer** to mix food together.

mop
A **mop** is used to clean the floor.

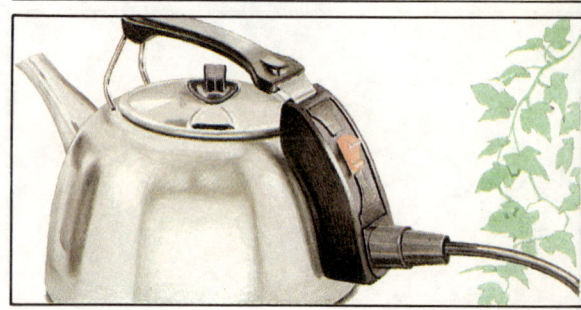

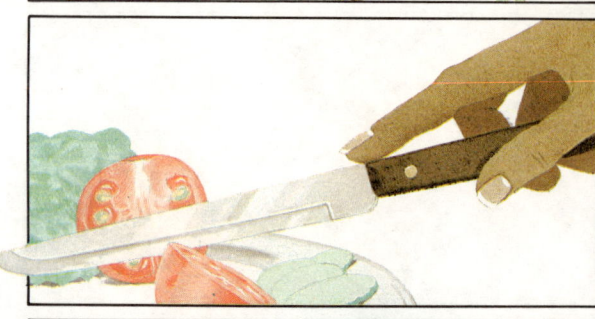

100

pan
You cook food in a **pan**.

plate
We eat food from a **plate**.

saucer
We put a **saucer** under a cup. It stops a hot cup from making marks on the table.

sink
We wash dishes in a **sink**. A **sink** has taps.

spoon
We eat soup, puddings and ice-cream with a **spoon**.

stool
A **stool** is a chair with no arms and no back.

kitchen

kitchen

table
A **table** has legs and a flat top. You eat at a **table**.

tap
We turn on the **tap** to get water. **Taps** with a red spot give hot water. **Taps** with a blue spot give cold water.

teapot
You make tea in a **teapot**.

tin
Some foods and drinks come in **tins**. We can open a **tin** with a **tin** opener.

toaster
We put bread in a **toaster** to make it hot and brown.

tumble drier
A **tumble drier** makes damp clothes dry.

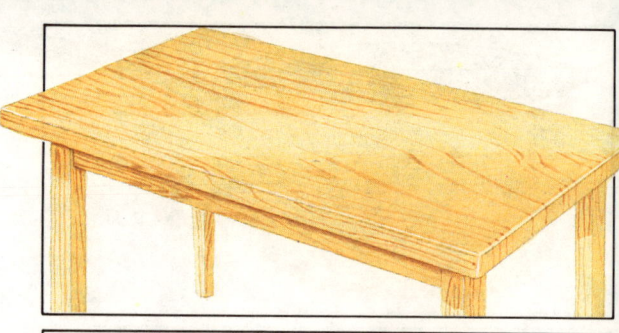

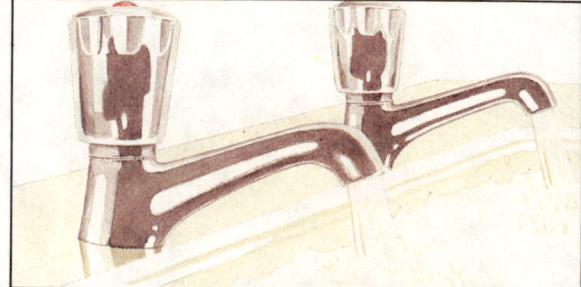

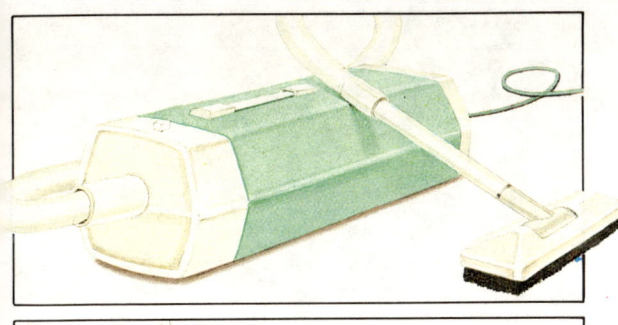

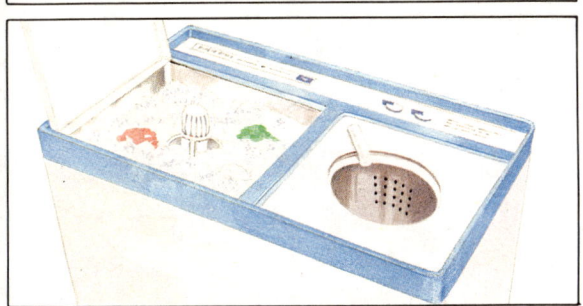

vacuum cleaner
A **vacuum cleaner** sucks up dirt from carpets and rugs.

washing machine
A **washing machine** makes dirty clothes clean.

waste bin
We put rubbish in a **waste bin**.

kitchen

living room

armchair
An **armchair** is a comfortable chair with sides and a back.

bookcase
We keep books in a **bookcase**.

carpet
A **carpet** makes the floor soft to walk on.

curtains
We hang **curtains** up at windows. At night, we close the **curtains**.

furniture
Chairs, tables and beds are **furniture**.

lamp
A **lamp** gives light. It uses electricity.

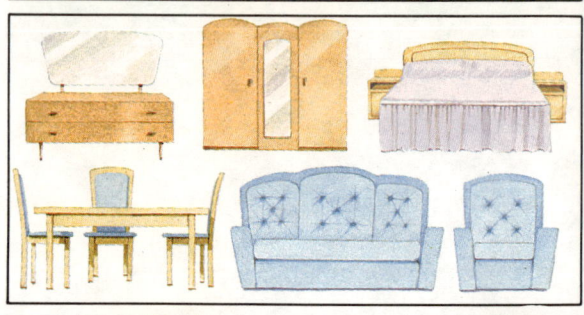

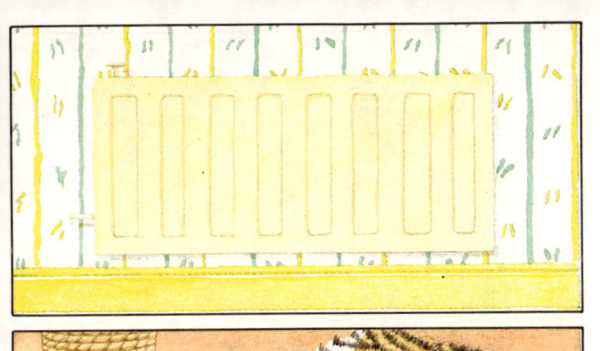

radiator
A **radiator** warms the room.

rug
A **rug** is a small carpet.

settee
A **settee** is a comfortable seat for more than one person.

sideboard
A **sideboard** has cupboards and drawers.

telephone
We can talk to people on a **telephone**. The people can be a long distance away.

television
We watch **television** at home.

living room

bathroom

bath
People wash in the **bath**.

flannel
We use a **flannel** to wash our face.

mirror
We can see ourselves in a **mirror**.

nail brush
We use a **nail brush** to clean our nails.

plug
A **plug** stops the water from running away.

shower
You can use a **shower** to wash your hair.

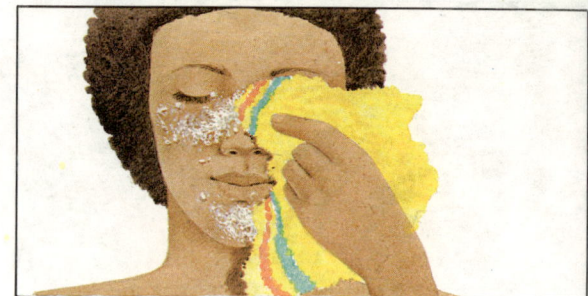

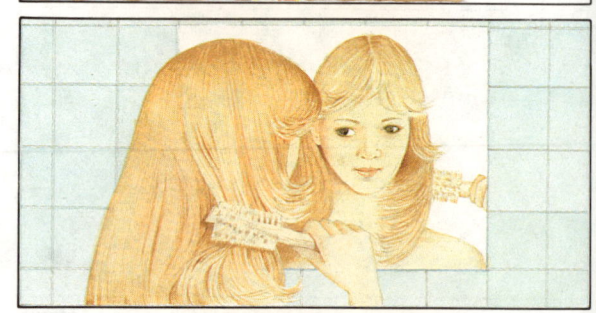

soap
We wash with **soap** and water.

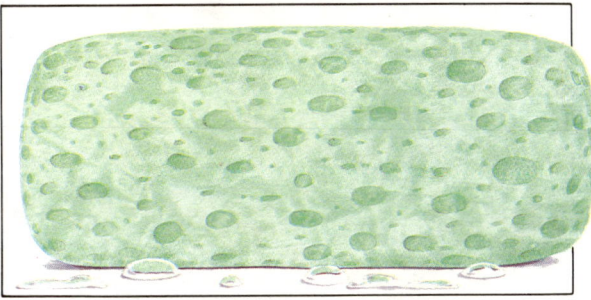

sponge
We can use a **sponge** in the bath. It holds a lot of water.

toilet
Toilets take away our body waste. We wash our hands after using the **toilet**.

toothbrush
We clean our teeth with a **toothbrush**.

towel
We use a **towel** to dry ourselves.

wash basin
We fill the **wash basin** with water to wash our hands and face.

bathroom

bedroom

bed
We go to sleep in a **bed**. It is warm and comfortable.

bunk bed
Bunk beds take up less room than two beds on the floor.

cot
A baby sleeps in a **cot**.

drawers
We keep clothes in a chest of **drawers**.

dressing table
You can keep your brush and comb on a **dressing table**. It often has a large mirror.

wardrobe
We hang our clothes in a **wardrobe**.

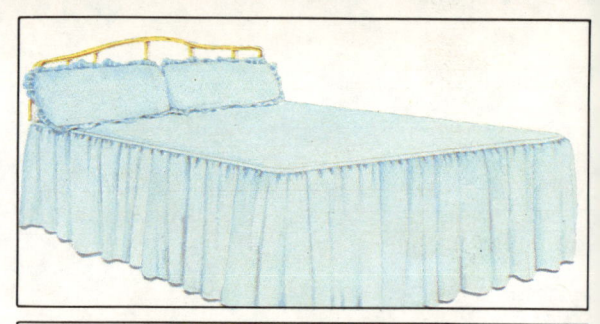

toys

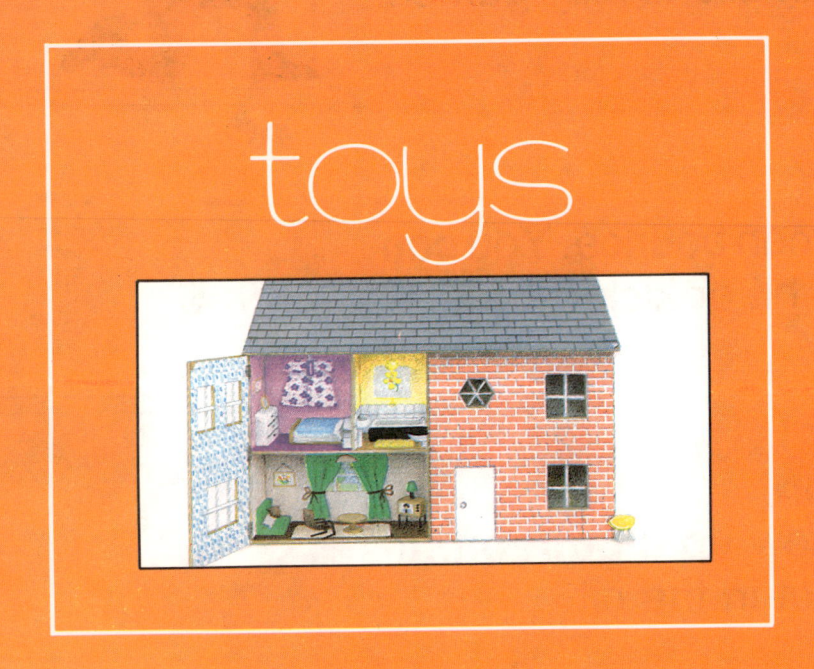

toys

Action Man
Action Man is a toy man you can use to play games.

ball
A **ball** can bounce. You can throw, hit or kick a **ball**.

balloon
You blow up a **balloon**. It will float in the air.

bat
You can hit a ball with a **bat**.

board
You play games on a **board**. We often throw dice to see how far we move on the **board**.

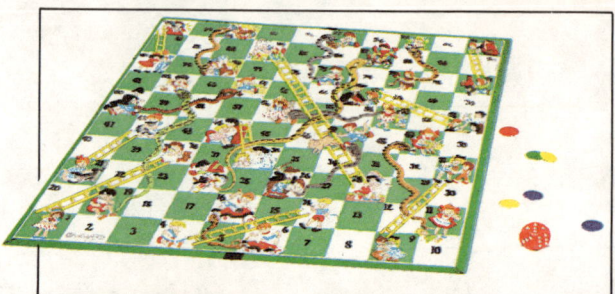

book
A **book** can tell a story. **Books** are also useful for looking up interesting things.

bricks
You can build a house with **bricks**.

car
You can pedal a toy **car** to make it move.

climbing frame
A **climbing frame** makes it easy to climb.

dice
You throw **dice** to play some games. The number of spots on the **dice** is the number of moves you must make.

doll
A **doll** is a toy baby, girl or boy.

doll's clothes
You can dress your doll with **doll's clothes**.

toys

toys

doll's house
A **doll's house** is a toy house for small dolls.

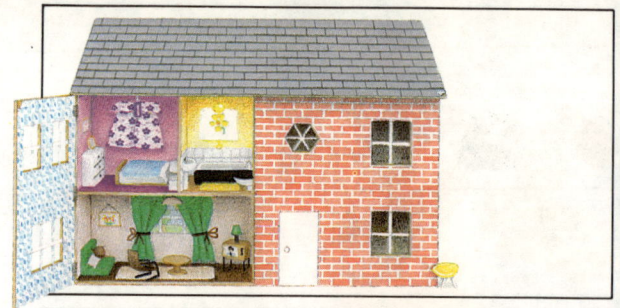

flag
We put a **flag** on top of the sand castle.

game
Snakes and ladders is a **game** you play on a board.

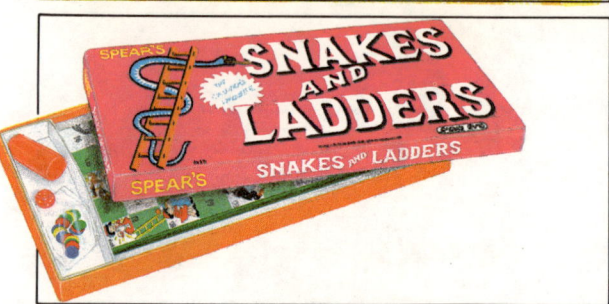

jigsaw
We fit the pieces of a **jigsaw** to make a picture.

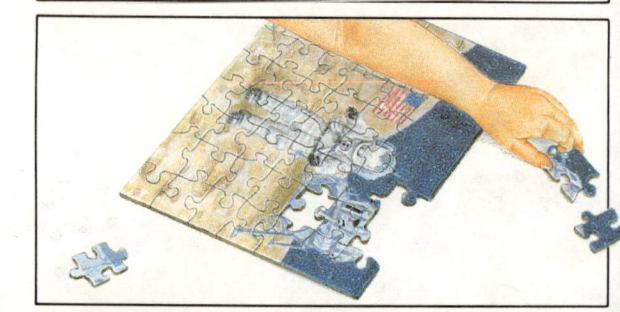

kite
We can fly a **kite** in the sky. The wind lifts it up.

marbles
Marbles are bright, glass balls. Children play **marbles** in the playground.

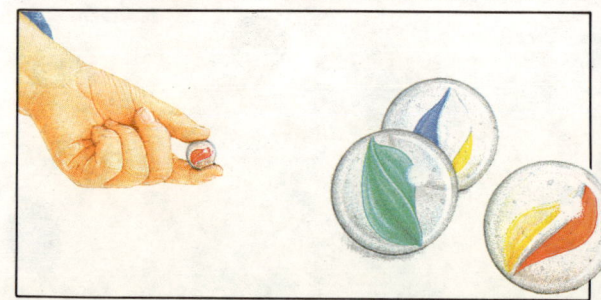

paints
A set of **paints** has lots of colours. We use a brush with **paints** to make pictures.

play people
You can use **play people** to play games like hospitals.

pram
You can push your doll along in a doll's **pram**.

puppet
A **puppet** is a doll you put on your hand to make it move. Some **puppets** are moved by strings.

roller skates
Roller skates have little wheels. You can move fast on your **roller skates**.

sand pit
A **sand pit** is full of sand for playing in.

toys

toys

seesaw
The children go up and down on the **seesaw**.

skipping rope
A **skipping rope** is a rope with handles for jumping over.

sledge
You can slide across the snow on a **sledge**.

slide
You sit on a **slide** and slip down to the ground.

swing
You sit on a **swing** and go backwards and forwards.

train set
A **train set** has an engine and coaches. They move on rails.

we use

we use

basket
We use a **basket** to carry things.

brush
We make hair tidy with a **brush**.

camera
A **camera** is used to take photographs.

cassette-recorder
We listen to music and stories on a **cassette-recorder**.

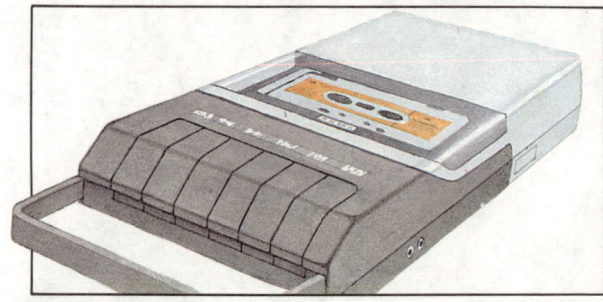

chalk
Chalk is used to write on a blackboard.

comb
A **comb** has teeth. It is used to make hair tidy.

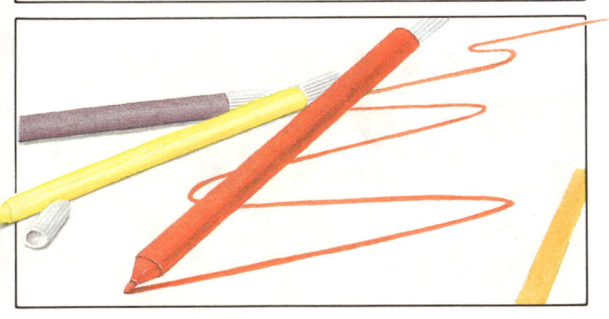

computer
We use a **computer** to help us learn. We can play games on our **computer**.

cushion
A **cushion** is a soft pillow for a chair.

felt tip
A **felt tip** is a pen used for writing and colouring.

guitar
A **guitar** is a musical instrument. It has six strings.

hairdrier
A **hairdrier** blows hot air. The hot air dries wet hair.

handbag
A **handbag** is a small bag used to hold things.

we use

we use

headphones
You can wear **headphones** to listen to records and cassettes.

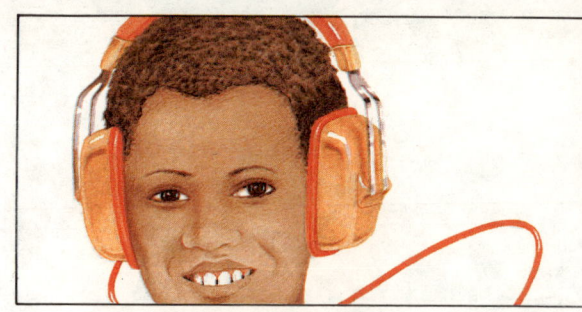

knitting needles
Knitting needles hold the stitches when we knit.

magazine
A **magazine** is a paper with stories and pictures.

magnet
A **magnet** will pick up pins and nails.

matches
We use **matches** to light fires. Never play with **matches**.

microphone
A **microphone** collects sound and passes it on a long way.

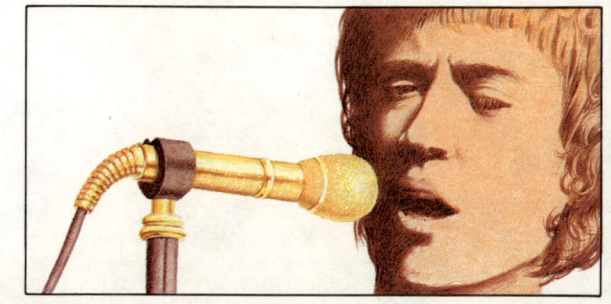

we use

money
Money is used to buy things.

needle
A **needle** is used for sewing.

newspaper
We read a **newspaper** to tell us what is happening.

organ
An **organ** is a musical instrument. It has keys like a piano.

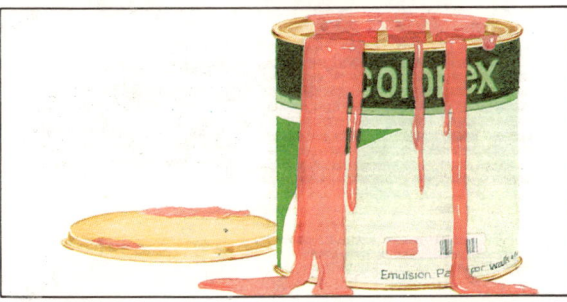

paint
We use **paint** to put colour on things. **Paint** also protects things from the weather.

paintbrush
You put on paint with a **paintbrush**.

we use

paper
We can write or draw on **paper** with a pen or pencil.

pencil
We use a **pencil** for drawing and writing.

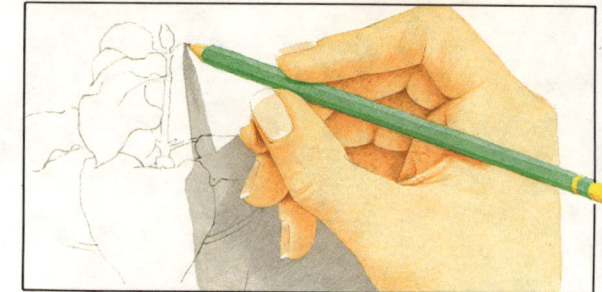

piano
A **piano** is a musical instrument. It has black keys and white keys.

purse
We carry money in a **purse**.

radio
We listen to the **radio** for news and music.

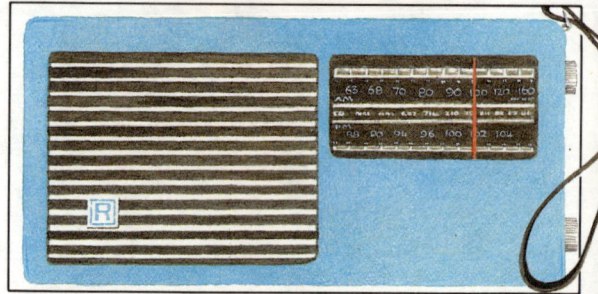

record-player
We play records on a **record-player**.

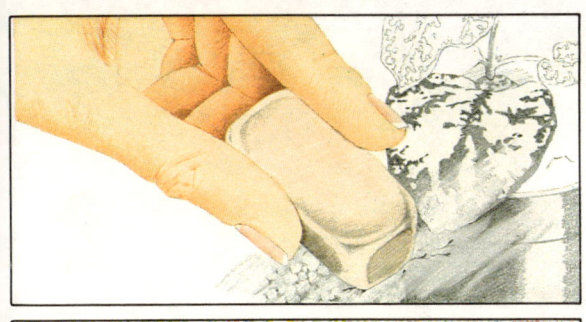

rubber
We use a **rubber** to remove pencil marks.

scissors
We can cut paper and cloth with **scissors**.

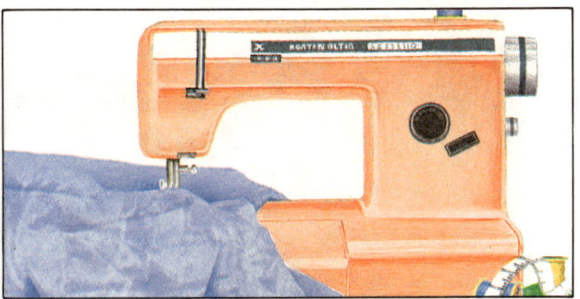

sewing machine
A **sewing machine** is used to sew and decorate material.

shopping bag
A **shopping bag** is used to carry shopping home.

supermarket trolley
A **supermarket trolley** holds the shopping we have to pay for.

toothbrush
You brush your teeth with a **toothbrush**.

we use

toothpaste
Toothpaste helps to keep your teeth clean. We squeeze the **toothpaste** onto a toothbrush.

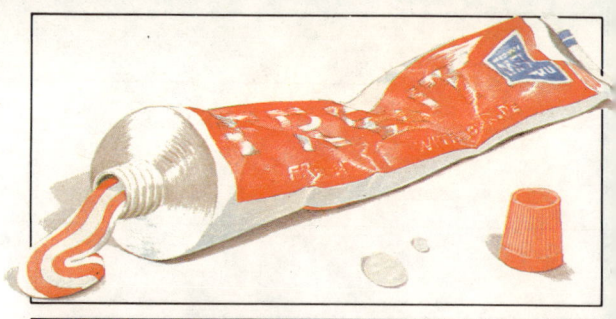

torch
A **torch** helps you to see things when it is dark.

umbrella
An **umbrella** keeps the rain off your head.

wallet
Money and cards are kept in a **wallet**.

washing line
We hang clothes on a **washing line** to dry.

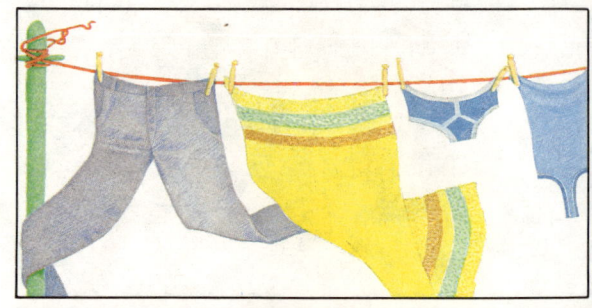

wool
We use **wool** when we knit. **Wool** comes from sheep.

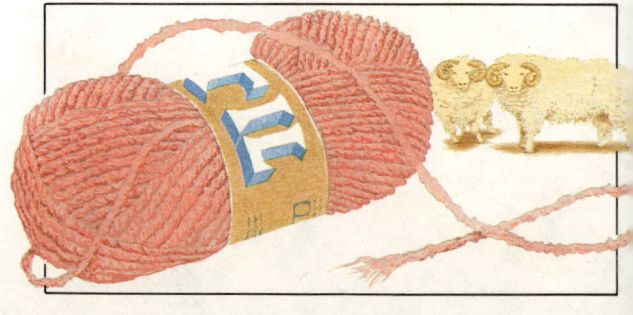

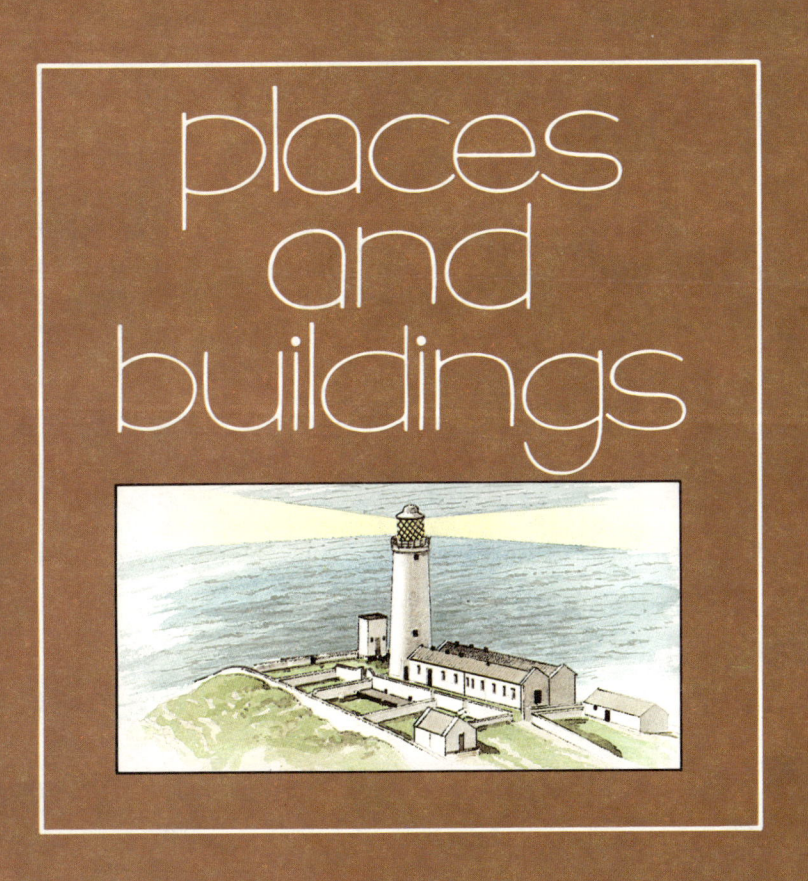

places and buildings

places and buildings

airport
Aeroplanes land and take off at an **airport**.

bakery
Bread, cakes and pies are made in a **bakery**.

beach
The **beach** is the sand and pebbles at the edge of the sea or a lake.

bungalow
A **bungalow** is a house with no upstairs.

bus station
People wait to catch buses at a **bus station**.

camp
A **camp** is where people sleep in tents.

canal
Ships and boats sail along a **canal**.

castle
A **castle** has walls round it. It was built to keep out enemies.

cave
A **cave** is a large hole in the earth or in a rock.

church
A **church** is where Christians pray to their God.

cinema
A **cinema** is where people watch films.

circus
A **circus** has animals, clowns and acrobats.

places and buildings

places and buildings

city
There are lots of buildings in a **city**. Many people live and work there.

corner
Two streets meet at a **corner**.

country
Fields, woods and farms are in the **country**.

earth
The **earth** is our home. The **earth** goes round the sun.

factory
A **factory** is where things are made.

fair
There are roundabouts, dodgems and sideshows at a **fair**.

places and buildings

farm
A **farm** is where cows, pigs, sheep and hens are kept. Food is grown on the **farm**.

field
A **field** is where some farm animals feed. Food is grown in some **fields**.

fire station
Fire engines are kept in the **fire station**.

flats
Flats are many homes in a tall building.

forest
A **forest** is where many trees grow.

garage
You can buy petrol and have your car repaired at a **garage**.

places and buildings

garden
Flowers, vegetables and grass can be grown in a **garden**.

harbour
A **harbour** is a safe place for boats and ships to stay.

hospital
People who are sick or hurt are cared for in a **hospital**.

hotel
A **hotel** has rooms for people to stay in.

house
A **house** is where people live.

island
An **island** is land that has water all round it.

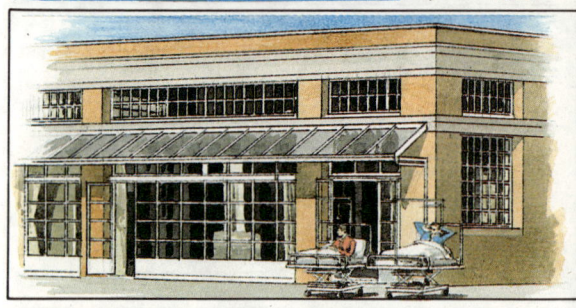

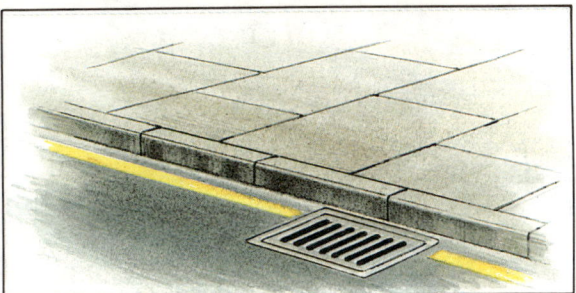

jungle
The **jungle** is hot and damp with lots of creepers and trees growing there. Many animals live in the **jungle**.

kerb
A **kerb** is at the edge of a pavement.

lake
A **lake** is water with land all around it.

library
Many books are kept in a **library**. You can borrow books from a **library**.

lighthouse
The light from the **lighthouse** warns ships to keep away from the rocks.

motel
A **motel** is like a hotel. It is used by people who travel in cars.

places and buildings

places and buildings

motorway
A **motorway** is a very wide and straight road used by cars, lorries and coaches.

mountain
A **mountain** is a very high hill.

museum
Many interesting things are kept in a **museum**.

observatory
People watch the stars from an **observatory**.

ocean
An **ocean** is a large sea. Most of the world is covered by **oceans**.

office
In an **office**, people usually work at their desk. Typists and clerks work in an **office**.

oil rig
An **oil rig** pumps out oil from under the sea.

palace
A king or queen lives in a **palace**.

park
A **park** has grass, flowers and trees. There is often a playground.

pavement
We walk safely on the **pavement** at the side of the road.

pelican crossing
It is safer to cross the road at the **pelican crossing**.

playground
A **playground** is where you play games and run about.

places and buildings

places and buildings

police station
A **police station** is where the police work.

post office
A **post office** is where you buy stamps and post letters and parcels.

restaurant
People go out and eat meals in a **restaurant**.

river
A **river** flows into the sea. It starts off as a stream in the mountains and hills.

road
Buses, cars, lorries and bicycles travel on a **road** to and from different places.

road signs
Road signs show drivers the way to different places. They also warn people to drive safely.

places and buildings

roundabout
A **roundabout** is at the middle of crossroads for traffic to go round.

school
Children go to **school** to learn.

seaside
At the **seaside** there are rocks, pebbles, sand and sea.

shop
A **shop** is where people buy things.

shopping centre
There are many shops in a **shopping centre**. Cars must be parked in the car park.

skating rink
People skate on ice at the **skating rink**.

133

places and buildings

skyscraper
A **skyscraper** is a very tall building in a city.

station
People get on and off trains at a **station**.

stream
A **stream** is a small river.

street
A **street** is a road in a town or city. **Streets** often have houses, shops and offices on both sides.

supermarket
A **supermarket** is a shop where you serve yourself.

swimming pool
People go to the **swimming pool** to swim.

theatre
A **theatre** is where shows are put on for many people to see and hear.

town
A **town** is smaller than a city.

traffic lights
Traffic lights show drivers when to stop and when to go.

valley
A **valley** is low land between two hills or mountains.

village
A **village** is much smaller than a town.

volcano
A **volcano** is a mountain with a hole at the top. Hot, liquid rock from inside the earth can escape through the hole.

places and buildings

places and buildings

wood
A **wood** is a small forest. Many different kinds of tree can grow in a **wood**.

world
The **world** is round. The **world** is the earth and all that is on it.

zebra crossing
It is safer to use a **zebra crossing** when you cross the road.

zoo
A **zoo** is where many different kinds of wild animals are kept.

transport

transport

aeroplane
An **aeroplane** has wings. It flies in the sky.

ambulance
An **ambulance** takes people to hospital.

bicycle
A **bicycle** has two wheels and two pedals. You sit on the saddle. Be careful when riding your **bicycle**.

boat
A **boat** sails on water.

bulldozer
A **bulldozer** moves earth or rubble.

bus
People pay to travel on a **bus**. It can carry many people to different places along its route.

car
We use a **car** to drive from place to place by road.

coach
A **coach** is a bus for special trips or long journeys.

crane
A **crane** is used to lift heavy things.

fire engine
The **fire engine** carries firemen to the fire.

helicopter
A **helicopter** is an aeroplane that does not have wings. It can hover in the sky.

hovercraft
The **hovercraft** can travel over land and sea. It floats on air.

transport

transport

hydrofoil
The **hydrofoil** skims across the water.

jeep
A **jeep** is a kind of car. It can travel over rough, bumpy ground.

jet plane
A **jet plane** can fly very high and very fast.

liner
A **liner** is a large ship that carries many people.

lorry
A **lorry** carries heavy loads by road.

moon buggy
A **moon buggy** is used by astronauts to travel on the moon.

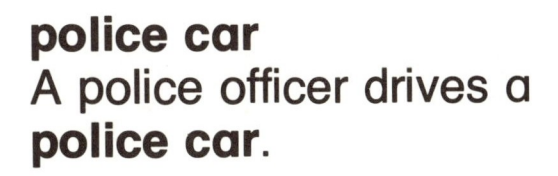

motor-bike
A **motor-bike** has two wheels and an engine. It can travel very fast.

police car
A police officer drives a **police car**.

rocket
A **rocket** blasts off into space.

ship
A **ship** sails on the sea.

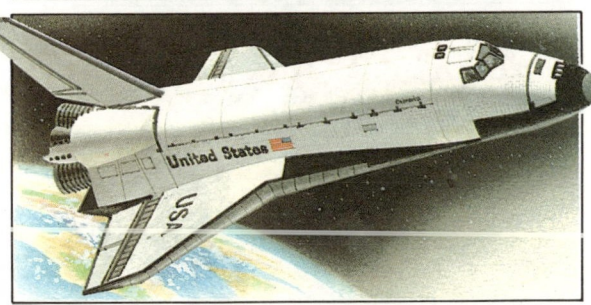

space shuttle
A **space shuttle** travels in space. It can land back on earth.

submarine
A **submarine** is a ship that can travel under the sea.

transport

transport

tanker
A **tanker** is a big lorry or ship which carries liquids. This **tanker** carries petrol.

taxi
People pay to travel in a **taxi**. It takes you where you want to go.

tractor
A farmer drives a **tractor**. It pulls a trailer.

train
A **train** travels on railway lines. **Trains** carry people and goods.

van
A **van** carries small loads. The post office **van** carries parcels.

yacht
A **yacht** has sails. The wind pushes it along.

action words

action words

answer
We **answer** the telephone when it rings.

bake
We **bake** bread in the oven to cook it.

begin
Daffodils **begin** to flower in the spring.

bend
Small trees **bend** in the wind.

bite
We **bite** an apple with our front teeth.

blow
We **blow** out the candles on our birthday cake.

144

bounce
Count how many times the ball can **bounce**.

break
If you drop an egg it will **break**.

brush
We **brush** our shoes to make them shine.

build
Workmen **build** houses.

button
You **button** up your coat to fasten it.

buy
We went to the shop to **buy** a book.

action words

action words

carry
We use a shopping bag to **carry** home the shopping.

catch
We **catch** the ball with both hands.

choose
We go to the library to **choose** a book.

chop
We **chop** wood with a chopper or axe.

clap
You **clap** your hands when you are pleased.

climb
Monkeys **climb** trees.

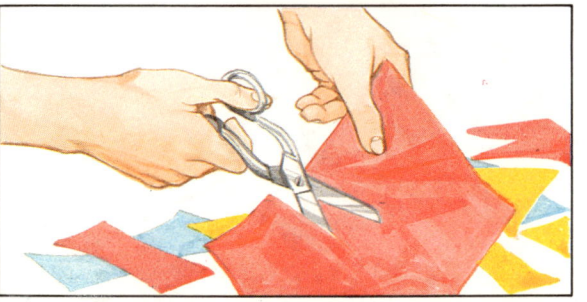

colour
You can use felt tips to **colour** a picture.

comb
We **comb** our hair to keep it tidy.

come
Some children **come** to school by bus.

crawl
Babies like to **crawl** on the floor.

cry
The boy began to **cry** when he fell off his bike.

cut
We **cut** paper with scissors.

action words

action words

cycle
Some children **cycle** to school.

dance
We **dance** in the hall at school.

dial
We **dial** 999 on the telephone when we need the police, fire engine or ambulance.

dig
People **dig** with spades.

dive
We learn to **dive** into a swimming pool.

drag
We **drag** our sledge up the hill.

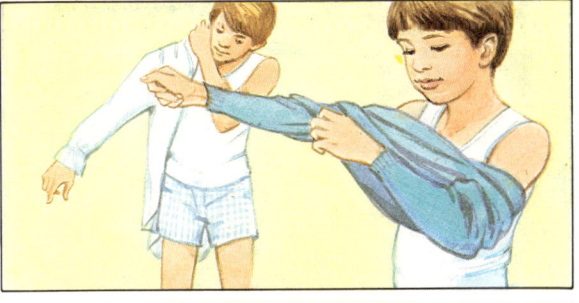

draw
We can **draw** pictures with a pencil.

dress
We **dress** ourselves when we get up in the morning.

drink
You can **drink** milk from a glass.

drive
The lady is learning to **drive** a car.

drop
If you **drop** a cup on the floor it will break.

eat
Cows **eat** grass when they are hungry.

action words

action words

fall
Leaves **fall** from the trees in the autumn.

feed
The children **feed** the ducks with bread.

fight
Sometimes dogs **fight** over a bone.

fill
You can **fill** your glass with milk.

fish
The children **fish** with a rod by the river.

fly
A bird uses wings to **fly**.

fold
We can help to **fold** the sheets.

follow
The cat likes to **follow** the girl to school.

freeze
The pond will **freeze** when it is very cold.

frown
We **frown** when the sun is in our eyes or when we are cross.

fry
We **fry** sausages in a pan.

give
We **give** presents on people's birthdays.

action words

action words

go
We **go** home from school in the afternoon.

grow
The kitten will **grow** into a cat.

hammer
When we mend a fence, we **hammer** nails into the wood.

hang
We **hang** the washing on the line to dry.

head
You can **head** the ball into the goal.

help
We like to **help** Mum to carry the shopping.

hide
We play **hide** and seek.

hit
You can **hit** a ball with a bat.

hop
The children **hop** on one leg in the playground.

hug
You **hug** with your arms.

iron
We **iron** our clothes to make them smooth.

jump
Horses can **jump** over fences.

action words

153

action words

kick
You can **kick** a ball a long way with your foot.

kiss
You **kiss** with your lips.

knit
Grandmother is going to **knit** a sweater.

knock
The postman will **knock** on the door.

laugh
We **laugh** when we watch clowns.

lie
We **lie** down in bed to go to sleep.

lift
Someone can **lift** you up to see.

meet
The boy and girl **meet** at the school gate.

mend
The man tries to **mend** the broken gate.

milk
The farmer showed us how to **milk** the cow.

mix
Our teacher asked us to **mix** the paints.

mop
When you spill milk you have to **mop** the floor.

action words

action words

move
We **move** our bodies in time to the music.

oil
We **oil** a bike to make it run smoothly.

open
We like to **open** our presents.

orbit
The spaceship began to **orbit** the moon. It travelled round it.

paddle
We like to **paddle** in the sea.

paint
You can use a big brush to **paint** this picture.

paste
You can **paste** pictures in your book.

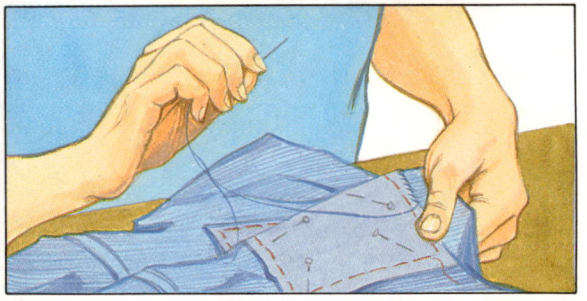

patch
Mum had to **patch** the hole in the trousers.

peel
You **peel** an orange before you eat it.

plant
We **plant** potatoes in our garden.

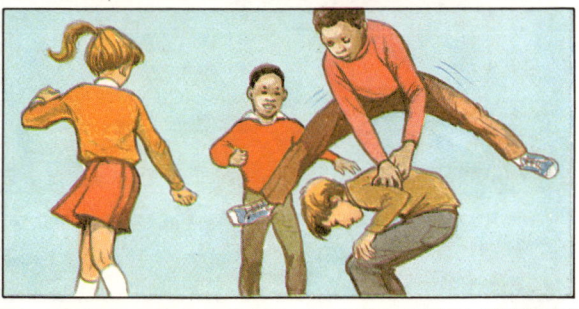

play
We have fun when we **play** in the playground.

point
Teacher asked the girl to **point** at the clock.

action words

action words

pour
You **pour** milk from a jug.

print
You can **print** your name neatly.

pull
You **pull** up weeds in the garden.

push
We all helped to **push** our car when it broke down.

put
You **put** the books on the shelf.

rain
When it begins to **rain**, we put up an umbrella.

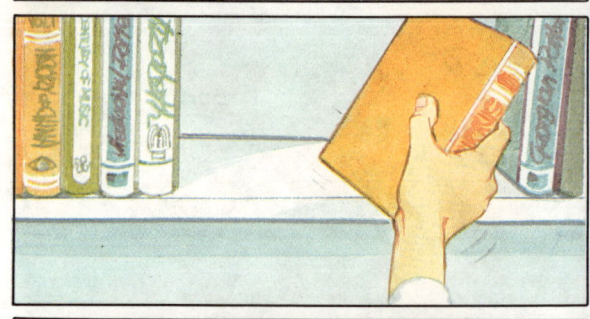

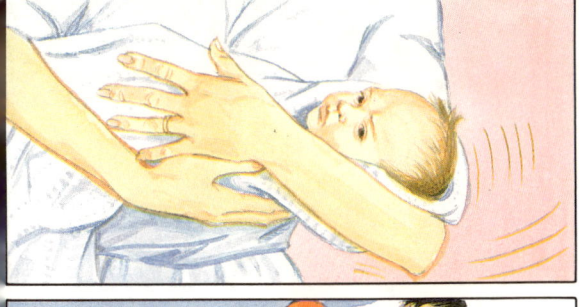

rake
We **rake** up the leaves in the garden.

ride
You can **ride** on a pony's back.

rise
We saw the balloon **rise** above the trees.

rock
Mum had to **rock** the baby to sleep.

roll
We like to **roll** snow into a big snowball.

run
You may have to **run** to catch a ball.

action words

action words

saw
We watched the man **saw** through the wood.

say
We **say** goodbye to our friends.

scare
A scarecrow will **scare** away birds.

see
We **see** a bird in the trees.

sew
You can **sew** a button on your shirt.

shake
The baby likes to **shake** his rattle.

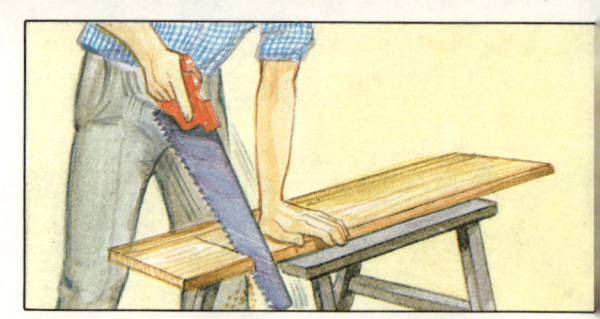

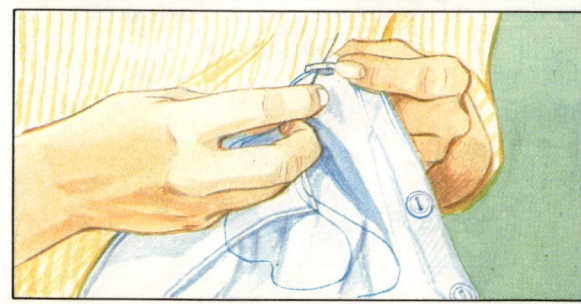

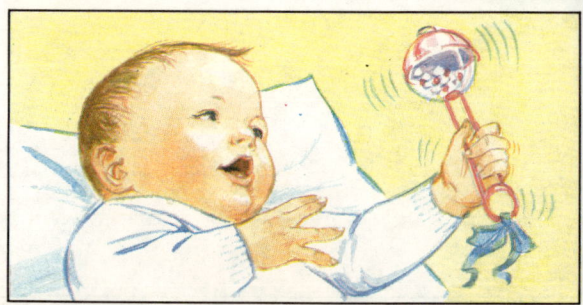

shout
You have to **shout** when there is a lot of noise.

show
He brought a puppy to **show** to his friend.

shut
We **shut** the window when it is raining.

sing
We **sing** songs at our concert.

sink
A stone will **sink** if you drop it in water.

sit
Grandfather likes to **sit** in the sun.

action words

action words

skate
We like to **skate** at the ice rink.

skip
We like to **skip** in the playground.

sleep
When we are tired we soon go to **sleep**.

slide
We **slide** down the hill on our sledge.

smile
You **smile** when you are happy.

snow
It began to **snow** on a cold night.

speak
We **speak** into the telephone.

spill
We saw the paint **spill** from the tin.

splash
We like to **splash** in the pool.

spread
You can **spread** butter on your toast.

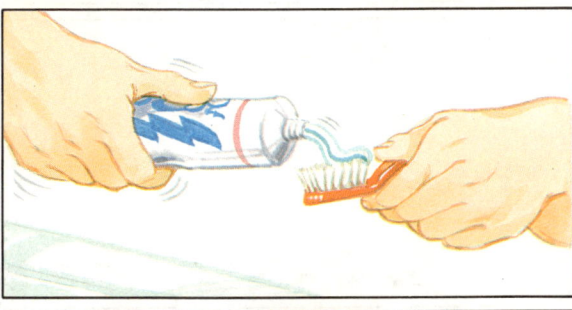

squeeze
You **squeeze** toothpaste on to your toothbrush.

stand
We **stand** at the bus stop.

action words

action words

step
The girl tried to **step** over the flowers.

stick
You **stick** a stamp on a postcard or letter.

stir
We **stir** tea with a spoon.

stop
The car had to **stop** at the crossing.

sweep
We use a brush to **sweep** the floor.

swim
We learn to **swim** a length of the pool.

swing
We **swing** in the park.

take
We **take** the dog for a walk.

talk
You **talk** to your friends when you tell them things.

tear
We **tear** the paper off a present.

tell
The policeman will **tell** us when to cross the road.

throw
You can **throw** a ball a long way.

action words

165

action words

tie
You **tie** your shoe laces in a bow.

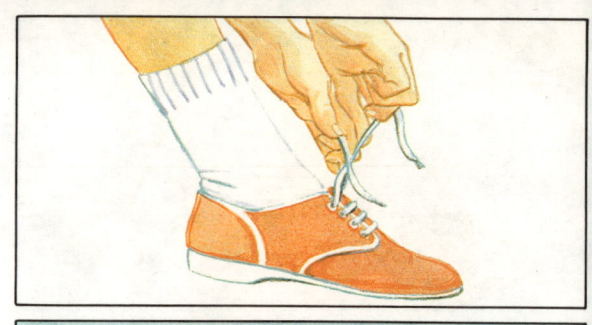

toast
We **toast** bread in the toaster.

touch
When you **touch** the cat it feels soft.

turn
We **turn** on the tap to wash our hands.

wake
You **wake** up when you hear the alarm clock.

walk
Many children **walk** to school.

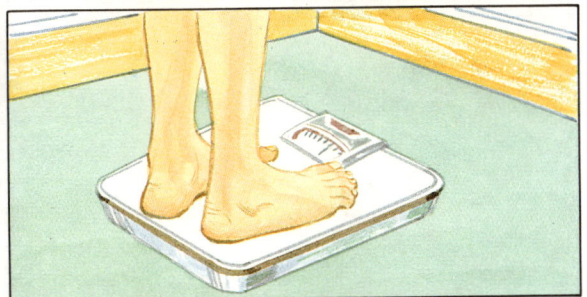

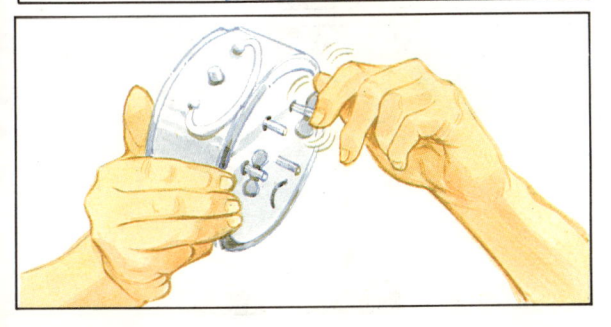

wash
We **wash** our hands before we eat.

watch
The children **watch** cartoons on television.

water
We **water** plants when the soil is dry.

weigh
You **weigh** yourself to find out how heavy you are.

whistle
We sometimes **whistle** when we are happy.

wind
You **wind** up a clock to make it work.

action words

action words

wink
We like to **wink** at our friends.

work
We **work** in the garden to look after the plants.

wrap
We like to **wrap** presents in pretty paper.

write
You can **write** your name in your exercise book.

yawn
We **yawn** when we are tired.

zip
You **zip** up your anorak.

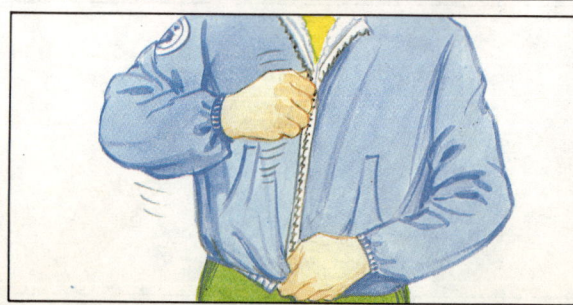

helpful words

helpful words

above
The aeroplane flew **above** the clouds.

at
The shop is **at** the corner of the street.

behind
The boys are hiding **behind** the wall.

below
The book is on the shelf **below** the flowers.

beside
The chair is **beside** the table.

between
The dog is **between** the children.

by
It is warm **by** the fire.

down
A spider is crawling **down** the wall.

from
The boy took a book **from** the shelf.

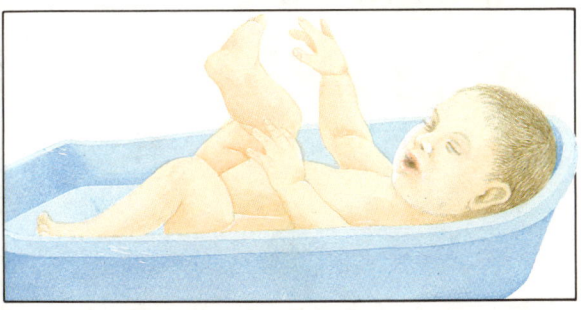

in
The baby is **in** the bath.

into
The dog went **into** his kennel.

off
The wind blew the man's hat **off** his head.

helpful words

where

on
The cat is **on** the roof.

outside
The children are playing **outside**.

over
The bridge goes **over** the river.

to
The people are going **to** the football match.

under
The dog is **under** the bed.

up
A squirrel is **up** the tree.

big
An elephant is a **big** animal.

clean
The car is **clean** after it has been washed.

cold
We wear more clothes on a **cold** day to keep warm.

dark
When it is **dark** we close the curtains.

dirty
We clean **dirty** shoes to make them shine.

dry
We put washing out on a line to make it **dry**.

what kind

what kind

funny
The **funny** clown made us laugh.

happy
There are many **happy** children at the party.

hot
Fire is **hot**.

left
This child holds his pencil in his **left** hand.

little
The robin is a **little** bird.

long
Father Christmas has a **long** beard.

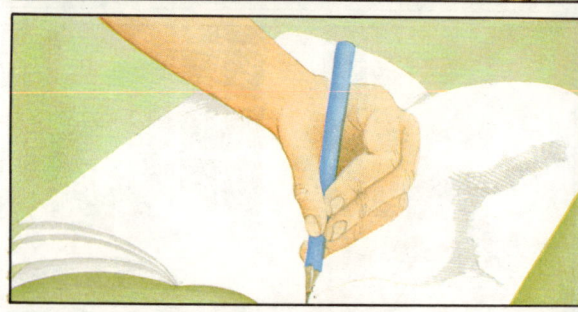

new
A **new** pair of shoes looks very clean.

old
The **old** car would not work.

right
This child holds her pencil in her **right** hand.

tall
A skyscraper is a **tall** building.

thin
We cut **thin** slices of bread to make sandwiches.

wet
The dog got **wet** in the water.

what kind

175

storybook people

storybook people

Aladdin
Aladdin rubbed his magic lamp.

Cinderella
Cinderella tried on the glass slipper.

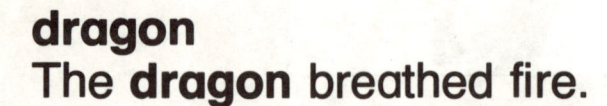

dragon
The **dragon** breathed fire.

dwarf
The **dwarf** is a very, very, small person. **Dwarfs** are busy people.

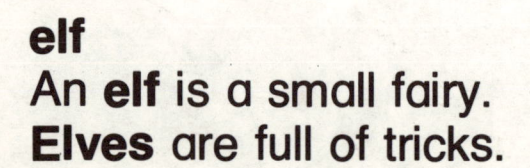

elf
An **elf** is a small fairy. **Elves** are full of tricks.

fairy
A **fairy** has a magic wand.

giant
A **giant** is very tall and strong.

goblin
A **goblin** is an ugly little man. **Goblins** are bad-tempered.

gold
Gold is a bright yellow metal. It is very precious.

Goldilocks
Goldilocks saw the three bears when she woke up.

storybook people

storybook people

Jack Frost
Jack Frost paints the windows with frost. Nobody ever sees him.

king
A **king** wears a gold crown. He sits on a throne.

knight
A **knight** wears armour and rides a horse.

magic
The **magic** carpet flew over the roof tops.

mermaid
A **mermaid** lives in the sea. She has long hair and a fish tail.

monster
A **monster** is an ugly creature. It frightens people.

ogre
An **ogre** is a horrible monster. It eats people.

pirate
A **pirate** steals from ships at sea.

prince
A **prince** is the son of a king or queen.

princess
A **princess** is the daughter of a king or queen.

storybook people

storybook people

Puss in Boots
Puss in Boots is a clever cat who wears large boots.

queen
A **queen** wears a gold crown. She lives in a palace.

Red Riding Hood
Red Riding Hood met a sly wolf. She was going to see her grandmother.

Snow White
Snow White lived with the Seven Dwarfs.

spell
A **spell** has magic powers. Witches and wizards make **spells** with frogs and lizards.

treasure
The pirates buried the **treasure**. They made a map of the place.

troll
The **troll** is a naughty dwarf. **Trolls** live in caves.

wand
A **wand** is a magic stick. It has a star on the end.

witch
The wicked **witch** cast a spell. **Witches** fly on broomsticks.

wizard
The **wizard** waved his wand. He can make magic.

storybook people

Monday

Tuesday

Solomon Grundy
Born on **Monday**,
Christened on **Tuesday**,
Married on **Wednesday**,
Took ill on **Thursday**,
Worse on **Friday**,
Died on **Saturday**,
Buried on **Sunday**,
This is the end,
Of Solomon Grundy.

Wednesday

Thursday

Friday

Saturday

Sunday

months

January
February
March
April
May
June
July
August
September
October
November
December

numbers

nought 0   **one** 1

two 2   **three** 3

four 4   **five** 5

six 6   **seven** 7

eight 8   **nine** 9

ten 10

afternoon

We go home from school in the **afternoon**.

half past

The postman collects the post at **half past** 5.

midnight

Midnight is 12 o'clock at night.

morning

We get up in the **morning**.

night

We sleep at **night**.

o'clock

School starts at 9 **o'clock**.

quarter past

The bus leaves at **quarter past** 10.

quarter to

The alarm went off at **quarter to** 8.

time

colours

black and white
A zebra is **black and white**.

blue
The **blue** jeans are drying on the line.

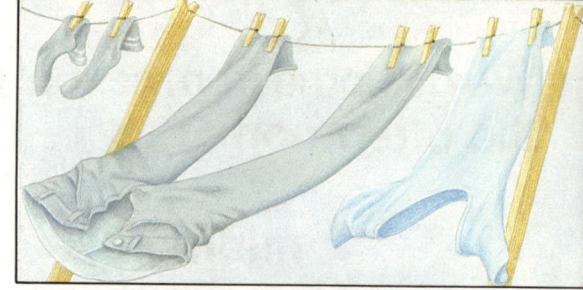

brown
The **brown** bear is big and fierce.

gold
This is a **gold** bar. It is a precious, yellow metal.

green
Peas are **green**.

grey
A **grey** squirrel is eating nuts.

orange
The fisherman is wearing an **orange** jacket.

pink
This party dress is **pink**.

purple
There are some **purple** flowers in the vase.

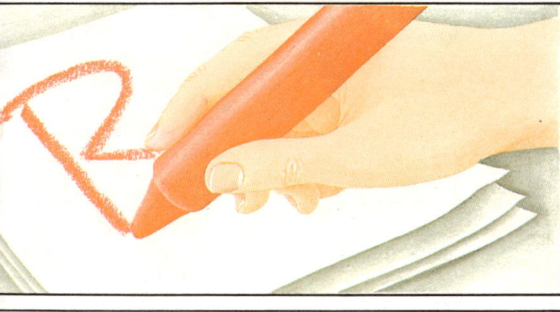

red
Here is a **red** wax crayon.

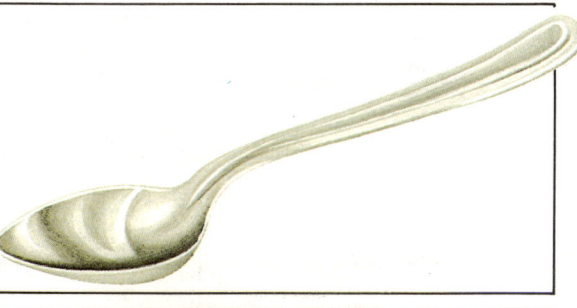

silver
This spoon is **silver**.

yellow
A sunflower is **yellow**.

colours

index

above, 170
acorn, 10
acrobat, 52
Action Man, 110
aerial, 92
aeroplane, 138
afternoon, 187
air hostess, 52
airport, 124
Aladdin, 178
alligator, 14
ambulance, 138
ankle, 44
anorak, 82
answer, 144
ant, 14
ape, 14
apple, 75
April, 185
apron, 82
arm, 44
armchair, 104
artist, 52
astronaut, 52
at, 170
athlete, 52
August, 185
aunt, 53
autumn, 6

baby, 53
bacon, 68
badger, 14
bake, 144
baker, 53
bakery, 124
ball, 110
balloon, 110
banana, 75
basket, 116
bat, 14, 110
bath, 106
beach, 124
beads, 82
bean, 78
bear, 15
beaver, 15
bed, 108
bee, 15
beef, 68
beetle, 15
beetroot, 78
begin, 144
behind, 170
below, 170
belt, 82
bend, 144
beside, 170
between, 170
bicycle, 94, 138
big, 173
bird, 15
bird table, 96
biscuit, 68
bison, 16
bite, 144
black and white, 188
blackbird, 16
blood, 44
blouse, 82
blow, 144
blue, 188
blue-tit, 16
board, 110
boat, 138
body, 44

bones, 44
book, 110
bookcase, 104
boots, 82
bounce, 145
boy, 53
bracelet, 83
brain, 45
bread, 68
break, 145
bricks, 111
bride, 53
bridegroom, 54
broccoli, 78
brontosaurus, 16
brother, 54
brown, 188
brush, 98, 116, 145
bucket, 98
budgerigar, 16
build, 145
bulb, 10
bulldozer, 138
bungalow, 124
bunk bed, 108
bus, 138
bush, 10
bus station, 124
butter, 68
butterfly, 17
button, 145
buy, 145
by, 171

cabbage, 78
cake, 68
calf, 17
camel, 17
camera, 116
camp, 124
canal, 125
canary, 17
cap, 83
car, 94, 111, 139
caravan, 94
cardigan, 83
carpet, 104
carrot, 78
carry, 146
cassette-recorder, 116
castle, 125
cat, 17
catch, 146
caterpillar, 18
cauliflower, 78
cave, 125
celery, 79
centipede, 18
chaffinch, 18
chair, 98
chalk, 116
cheese, 69
cherry, 75
chest, 45
chickens, 18
child, 54
chimney, 92
chimpanzee, 18
chip, 69
chocolate, 69
choose, 146
chop, 146
church, 125
Cinderella, 178
cinema, 125
circus, 125

city, 126
clap, 146
clean, 173
climb, 146
climbing frame, 111
cloud, 6
clown, 54
coach, 139
coat, 83
cockerel, 19
coffee, 69
coffee pot, 98
cold, 173
colour, 147
comb, 116, 147
come, 147
computer, 117
cone, 69
conker, 10
cook, 54
cooker, 98
corner, 126
cornflakes, 69
cot, 108
country, 126
cousin, 55
cow, 19
cowboy, 55
crab, 19
crane, 139
crawl, 147
crocodile, 19
crow, 19
crowd, 55
cry, 147
cub, 20
cucumber, 79
cup, 98
cupboard, 99
curtains, 104
cushion, 117
custard, 70
cut, 147
cycle, 148

dad, 55
daddy long legs, 20
dance, 148
dark, 173
daughter, 55
December, 185
deer, 20
dentist, 56
dial, 148
dice, 111
dig, 148
dinosaur, 20
dirty, 173
dive, 148
diver, 56
doctor, 56
dog, 20
doll, 111
doll's clothes, 111
doll's house, 112
dolphin, 21
donkey, 21
door, 92
dormouse, 21
down, 171
drag, 148
dragon, 178
dragonfly, 21
drain, 92
draw, 149
drawers, 108

dress, 83, 149
dressing gown, 83
dressing table, 108
drink, 149
drive, 149
driver, 56
drop, 149
dry, 173
duck, 21
dustman, 56
dwarf, 178

eagle, 22
ears, 45
earth, 126
earwig, 22
eat, 149
egg, 70
eight, 186
elbow, 45
electrician, 57
elephant, 22
elf, 178
emu, 22
eyes, 45

face, 46
factory, 126
fair, 126
fairy, 179
fall, 150
family, 57
farm, 127
farmer, 57
father, 57
February, 185
feed, 150
feet, 46
felt tip, 117
fence, 92
field, 127
fight, 150
fill, 150
fingers, 46
fire engine, 139
fireman, 57
fire station, 127
fish, 22, 150
fish finger, 70
five, 186
flag, 112
flannel, 106
flats, 127
flower, 10
fly, 23, 150
foal, 23
fog, 6
fold, 151
follow, 151
football boots, 84
footballer, 58
forest, 127
fork, 96, 99
four, 186
fox, 23
freeze, 151
freezer, 99
Friday, 184
fridge, 99
frog, 23
from, 171
frost, 6
frown, 151
fry, 151
funny, 174
furniture, 104

game, 112
garage, 92, 127
garden, 96, 128
gate, 93
gerbil, 23
giant, 179
giraffe, 24
girl, 58
give, 151
glass, 99
gloves, 84
go, 152
goat, 24
goblin, 179
gold, 179, 188
goldfish, 24
Goldilocks, 179
goose, 24
gorilla, 24
grandchild, 58
grandfather, 58
grandmother, 58
grape, 75
grapefruit, 75
grass, 11
grasshopper, 25
grass snake, 25
green, 188
greenhouse, 96
grey, 188
grow, 152
guinea pig, 25
guitar, 117
guppy, 25

hair, 46
hairband, 84
hairdresser, 59
hairdrier, 117
half past, 187
hamburger, 70
hammer, 94, 152
hamster, 25
hand, 46
handbag, 117
hang, 152
happy, 174
harbour, 128
hare, 26
hat, 84
head, 47, 152
headphones, 118
heart, 47
hedgehog, 26
heel, 47
helicopter, 139
help, 152
hen, 26
heron, 26
herring, 26
hide, 153
hippopotamus, 27
hit, 153
honey, 70
hop, 153
horse, 27
hose, 96
hospital, 128
hot, 174
hot dog, 70
hotel, 128
house, 128
hovercraft, 139
hug, 153
husband, 59
hydrofoil, 140

190

index

ice, 6
ice-cream, 71
in, 171
insect, 27
into, 171
iron, 99, 153
ironing board, 100
island, 128

jack, 94
jacket, 84
Jack Frost, 180
jam, 71
January, 185
jay, 27
jeans, 84
jeep, 140
jelly, 71
jet plane, 140
jigsaw, 112
jug, 100
July, 185
jump, 153
jumper, 85
June, 185
jungle, 129

kangaroo, 27
kerb, 129
kettle, 100
kick, 154
kid, 28
king, 180
kingfisher, 28
kiss, 154
kite, 112
kitten, 28
knee, 47
knife, 100
knight, 180
knit, 154
knitting needles, 118
knock, 154
koala bear, 28

ladder, 94
lady, 59
ladybird, 28
lake, 129
lamb, 29, 71
lamp, 104
laugh, 154
leaf, 11
leek, 79
left, 174
legs, 47
lemon, 75
lemonade, 71
leopard, 29
letterbox, 93
librarian, 59
library, 129
lie, 154
lift, 155
lighthouse, 129
lightning, 6
liner, 140
lion, 29
little, 174
lizard, 29
lobster, 29
lollipop, 71
long, 174
lorry, 140

magazine, 118
magic, 180
magnet, 118
man, 59
marbles, 112
March, 185
marmalade, 72
marrow, 79
matches, 118
May, 185
meat, 72
mechanic, 60
meet, 155
melon, 76
mend, 155
mermaid, 180
microphone, 118
midnight, 187
milk, 72, 155
milk shake, 72
miner, 60
mirror, 106
mittens, 85
mix, 155
mixer, 100
mole, 30
Monday, 184
money, 119
monkey, 30
monster, 181
moon, 7
moon buggy, 140
mop, 100, 155
morning, 187
mosquito, 30
motel, 129
moth, 30
mother, 60
motor-bike, 141
motorway, 130
mountain, 130
mouse, 30
mouth, 48
move, 156
mower, 96
muscles, 48
museum, 130
mushroom, 79

nail, 48
nail brush, 106
nails, 95
neck, 48
needle, 119
neighbour, 60
nephew, 60
nesting box, 97
new, 175
newspaper, 119
newt, 31
niece, 61
night, 187
nightdress, 85
nine, 186
nose, 48
nought, 186
November, 185
nurse, 61

observatory, 130
ocean, 130
o'clock, 187
October, 185
octopus, 31
off, 171
office, 130

ogre, 181
oil, 156
oil rig, 131
old, 175
on, 172
one, 186
onion, 79
open, 156
orange, 76, 189
orange juice, 72
orbit, 156
organ, 119
otter, 31
outside, 172
over, 172
owl, 31

paddle, 156
paint, 119, 156
paintbrush, 119
painter, 61
paints, 113
palace, 131
pan, 101
pancake, 72
panda, 31
pants, 85
paper, 120
parents, 61
park, 131
parrot, 32
paste, 157
patch, 157
pavement, 131
pea, 80
peach, 76
peacock, 32
pear, 76
peel, 157
pelican crossing, 131
pencil, 120
pendant, 85
penguin, 32
people, 61
pepper, 80
person, 62
photographer, 62
piano, 120
pie, 73
pig, 32
pigeon, 32
piglet, 33
pilot, 62
pinafore dress, 85
pineapple, 76
pink, 189
pirate, 181
plant, 11, 157
plate, 101
play, 157
playground, 131
play people, 113
plimsolls, 86
plug, 106
plum, 76
plumber, 62
point, 157
polar bear, 33
police car, 141
policeman, 62
police station, 132
policewoman, 63
pony, 33
porcupine, 33
pork, 73
postman, 63

post office, 132
potato, 80
pour, 157
pram, 113
prawn, 33
prince, 181
princess, 181
print, 158
pudding, 73
pull, 158
puppet, 113
puppy, 34
purple, 189
purse, 120
push, 158
Puss in Boots, 182
put, 158
pyjamas, 86

quarter past, 187
quarter to, 187
queen, 182
queue, 63

rabbit, 34
radiator, 105
radio, 120
rain, 7, 158
rainbow, 7
raincoat, 86
rake, 97, 159
raspberry, 77
rat, 34
record-player, 120
red, 189
Red Riding Hood, 182
reindeer, 34
relatives, 63
restaurant, 132
rhinoceros, 34
rhubarb, 77
ribbon, 86
ride, 159
right, 175
ring, 86
rise, 159
river, 132
road, 132
road signs, 132
robin, 35
rock, 159
rocket, 141
roll, 159
roller skates, 113
roof, 93
rook, 35
roots, 11
roundabout, 133
rubber, 121
rug, 105
run, 159

sailor, 63
sandals, 86
sand pit, 113
sandwich, 73
Saturday, 184
saucer, 101
sausage, 73
sausage roll, 73
saw, 95, 160
say, 160
scare, 160
scarf, 87
school, 133
scissors, 121

screwdriver, 95
screws, 95
seagull, 35
seahorse, 35
seal, 35
seaside, 133
see, 160
seeds, 11
seesaw, 114
September, 185
settee, 105
seven, 186
sew, 160
sewing machine, 121
shake, 160
shark, 36
shed, 97
sheep, 36
shepherd, 64
ship, 141
shirt, 87
shoes, 87
shop, 133
shopkeeper, 64
shopping bag, 121
shopping centre, 133
shoulders, 49
shout, 161
show, 161
shower, 106
shut, 161
sideboard, 105
silver, 189
sing, 161
sink, 101, 161
sister, 64
sit, 161
six, 186
skate, 162
skating rink, 133
skin, 49
skip, 162
skipping rope, 114
skirt, 87
sky, 7
skyscraper, 134
sledge, 114
sleep, 162
slide, 114, 162
smile, 162
snail, 36
snake, 36
snow, 7, 162
Snow White, 182
soap, 107
socks, 87
soldier, 64
son, 64
soup, 74
space, 7
space shuttle, 141
spade, 97
spanner, 95
sparrow, 36
speak, 163
spell, 182
spider, 37
spill, 163
splash, 163
sponge, 107
spoon, 101
spread, 163
spring, 8
sprout, 80
squeeze, 163
squirrel, 37

index

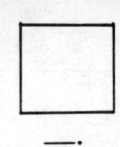

stand, 163
star, 65
starfish, 37
stars, 8
station, 134
stegosaurus, 37
step, 93, 164
stick, 164
stickleback, 37
stir, 164
stoat, 38
stomach, 49
stool, 101
stop, 164
strawberry, 77
stream, 134
street, 134
submarine, 141
suit, 87
summer, 8
sun, 8
Sunday, 184
supermarket, 134
supermarket trolley, 121
swallow, 38
swan, 38
sweater, 88
sweep, 164
sweet, 74
sweetcorn, 80
swim, 164
swimming pool, 134
swimsuit, 88
swing, 114, 165

table, 102
take, 165
talk, 165
tall, 175
tangerine, 77
tanker, 142
tap, 102
taxi, 142
tea, 74
teacher, 65
teapot, 102
tear, 165
teeth, 49
telephone, 105
television, 105
tell, 165
ten, 186
theatre, 135
thin, 175
three, 186
throat, 49
throw, 165
thrush, 38
thumb, 50
thunder, 8
Thursday, 184
tie, 88, 166
tiger, 38
tights, 88
tin, 102
to, 172
toad, 39
toadstool, 12
toast, 74, 166

toaster, 102
toes, 50
toilet, 107
tomato, 77
toothbrush, 107, 121
toothpaste, 122
torch, 122
tortoise, 39
touch, 166
towel, 107
town, 135
tractor, 142
traffic lights, 135
train, 142
trainers, 88
train set, 114
treasure, 183
trees, 12
troll, 183
trousers, 88
trowel, 97
trunks, 89
t-shirt, 89
Tuesday, 184
tumble drier, 102
turkey, 39
turn, 166
turnip, 80
turtle, 39
twin, 65
two, 186
typist, 65
tyrannosaurus rex, 39
tyres, 95

umbrella, 122
uncle, 65
under, 172
underpants, 89
up, 172

vacuum cleaner, 103
valley, 135
van, 142
vest, 89
vet, 66
village, 135
volcano, 135

waist, 50
waiter, 66
waitress, 66
wake, 166
walk, 166
wall, 93
wallet, 122
walrus, 40
wand, 183
wardrobe, 108
wash, 167
wash basin, 107
washing line, 122
washing machine, 103
wasp, 40
waste bin, 103
watch, 89, 167
water, 74, 167
Wednesday, 184
weigh, 167

wellingtons, 89
wet, 175
whale, 40
wheelbarrow, 97
whistle, 167
wife, 66
wildcat, 40
wind, 167
window, 93
wink, 168
winter, 8
witch, 183
wizard, 183
wolf, 40
woman, 66
wood, 136
woodlouse, 41
woodpecker, 41
wool, 122
work, 168
world, 136
worm, 41
wrap, 168
wrist, 50
write, 168

yacht, 142
yawn, 168
yellow, 189
yoghurt, 74

zebra, 41
zebra crossing, 136
zip, 168
zoo, 136